Anonymous

Albuquerque Business Directory for 1883

Anonymous

Albuquerque Business Directory for 1883

ISBN/EAN: 9783337219178

Printed in Europe, USA, Canada, Australia, Japan

Cover: Foto ©Suzi / pixelio.de

More available books at **www.hansebooks.com**

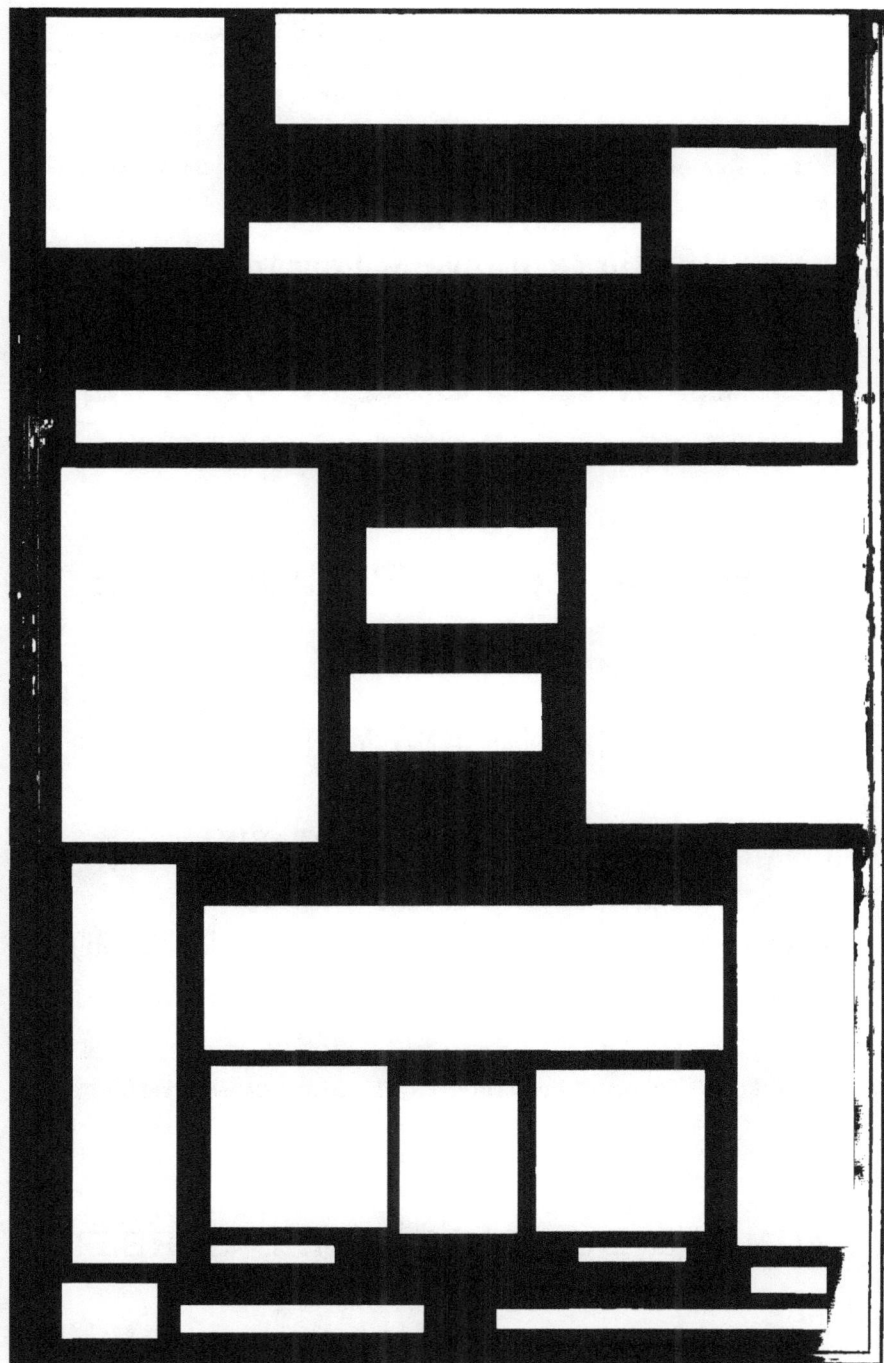

MARIANO ARMIJO.   ELIAS ARMIJO.   JOHN BORRADAILE.

Armijo Brothers & Borradaile

REAL ESTATE

——AND——

Bernalillo County Abstract Office

→MINES, INSURANCE AND MONEY BROKERS←

CONVEYANCERS AND NOTARIES.

Deeds Executed in either the English or Spanish Language

Take full Charge of Properties, Pay Taxes and Collect Rents.

MUNROE BUILDING, THIRD STREET

ALBUQUERQUE, N. M.

PREFACE.

THE City of Albuquerque has reached a point of commercial development at which her origin and history have become of more than passing interest, and which renders statistics of her business and progress a safe basis for calculations for the future, in social, commercial and political points of view.

That New Mexico is destined soon to enter the family of sovereign states, which constitute the American union, and that Albuquerque is to be the social, political and commercial center of the new state, are generally recognized certainties of the near future. It is with a full appreciation of these facts that I entered upon the preparation and publication of this book.

It has been prepared with great and careful painstaking and research, that every statement of fact should be reliable, and every inference legitimate, and the initiatory step to the presentation of all the essential facts of the past, present and future history of the city, and in some sense, of the territory.

In this connection I desire to acknowledge the kindness of Judge Hazeldine and Prof. Bryan for the use of records from which was drawn much of the information herein contained ; also, to Father Durante, for the translation of the statement of José Lucero, sacristan of the church in the West End, whose father, for many years before, held the same office in the old structure that preceded the present one.

José Lucero says that his father and himself, for many years, owned the book from which were drawn many of the facts of the earliest history of this city and the territory. That book is now lost, but he destinctly remembers often reading it, and the statements of the journeyings and discoveries, and the founding of colonies and cities by the first governor, Don Juan de U ñate, herein related.

Although it is a settled point in the minds of the intelligent people, that this place has had a history in the past, that which is herein written is what remains, though meagre, yet may be of interest and importance to the generous people of this city and community, to whom this work is dedicated.

With sentiments of profound respect,

JOHN H. SULLIVAN.

JOHN J. PHELAN

Wholesale and Retail Dealer in

Drugs and Druggists' Sundries

PAINTS, OILS

VARNISHES AND BRUSHES

Soaps, Perfumes and Toilet Articles

—THE—

Largest and Most Complete Stock

IN THE TERRITORY

Prescription Counter Open Day and Night

☞Orders from a distance solicited. Prompt attention and satisfaction guaranteed.

Corner Railroad Avenue and Second Street

ALBUQUERQUE, N. M.

ALBUQUERQUE.*

BETWEEN 1540 and 1550 is the date of the first recorded presence of Europeans in this locality. Sometime during these years, in the reign of Ferdinand VII, King of Spain, Don Juan de Uñate was commissioned the first governor of the province of New Mexico. On his route to his new jurisdiction Gov. Uñate passed through Chihuahua and El Paso northwesterly to pueblo Zuñi, in the western part of the now territory of New Mexico, apparently in search of a place for headquarters to the province. The record states that to these people he offered friendship, civilization and the catholic religion. He left with them a priest and several families. From there he turned eastward to pueblo Laguna, wheré he also left a priest and a few families. From Laguna his route led him to Isleta, where he left a Fanciscan father and some families. From Isleta he followed up the river, which he is supposed to have named the Rio Grande del Norte, by reason of it being the first large river he had met on his northward journey from the city of Mexico. Arriving immediately opposite where the present town of Albuquerque is located, he found a village on the west bank of the river, which must then have been of considerable importance, as the ruins can yet be traced on the bank of the river for more than a mile in extent. These ruins plainly define its location and indicates its size.

On the east bank of the river where Albuquerque now stands, were a few occupied houses, the ruins of which can yet be seen. Here a military post was established and garrisoned with 500 soldiers, and named the post Presidio de Albuquerque. Here he also left a Franciscan father and several Spanish and Mexican families. After some delay in regulating the new post and settlement, Gov. Uñate resumed his journey of observation and discovery, going in a northerly direction, and in due time arrived at what he found to be the largest pueblo in the province—now the historic city of Santa Fe. Here he established his headquarters and the seat of provincial government. From this point and base of oper-

*White Oak.

ations he made occasional journeys over the province, establishing the Spanish authority and missionary stations.

In the year of 1659, history informs us that Francisco Fernandez de la Cueva, Duke of Albuquerque, ruled in this country as viceroy of Mexico to the expiration of 1660. Now appears the name of San Filipe de Albuquerque, and in a few years, by edict of the King of Spain, it was declared a ville (city), and from that circumstance it is a legitimate inference that it was a place of importance. Another and more conclusive proof that such was the fact is, that in the archives of this territory, in the city of Mexico, has been found the registry of the church at this place, in which are registered the names of 4031 persons as belonging to the catholic communion here in 1698, nearly equally divided, male and female ; so to allow one non-communicant for each communicant, would make a population of at least 8000 souls at that time.

In the year 1701 the Duke of Albuquerque returned to this country as governor. He was reputed a good man of great justice, and while just, was also a kind and human ruler. As an evidence of the estimation in which he was held by his people, the ville (or city,) was named Albuquerque in the year of 1703. His administration continued in this country until during the year 1711, when he ceased to rule here.

If there was, as many suppose, and not without good reason, a settlement of the native population at this place prior to 1550, it is not given in any tangible form or authentic history. Such opinion has to rest entirely upon tradition, which, however, is of such a character that it is not at all unworthy of credit. Another very important fact which goes far to prove the long ago importance of this location to the Aztec population, ante-dating the presence of the Spaniards, is this, all the ancient roads of the country converge at this crossing of the river and center in this fertile valley, where the people came, not unlike those who are coming now to this same place, where their best interests can be developed and their comfort promoted.

The reasonable conclusion of the matter is, that far beyond where the memory of man begins, or knoweth anything to the contrary, in this valley a prosperous people lived and sought their highest welfare—just as we are doing now. The city is in the beautiful valley on the eastern shore of the Rio del Norte, or the Rio Grande of to-day, on the 35th parallel north latitude, 4918 feet above the sea level, with a mild and balmy climate, very healthy ; so much so, that many invalids have visited this place, most of whom have been greatly benefited, while others have been entirely restored in health.

The valley is wonderfully fertile, producing almost every variety of grain, vegetables and fruits of large size and in enormous quantities, of most delicious flavor, nutricious and health giving.

The crops are uniform in their yield, as most of them require irrigation, which, when done, insures an abundant return for the labor, which is less than is necessary in the states, where farmers are generally satisfied with one-third to one-half the quantity harvested by the well-to-do farmers in these valleys. An ample supply of water can be had and conducted to the arable lands for purposes of irrigation, throughout the extent of the valleys.

This location has long been a place of much importance ; equally so to four distinct nationalities—Aztec, Spain, Mexico and the United States, under which latter government all its capabilities will, most likely, soon be fully developed.

Under the auspicies of the New Mexico Town Company, the new portion of the town was laid out on the west and east sides of the Atchison, Topeka & Santa Fe railroad track during the early part of the year of 1880. The two first lots were .sold to Maden Brothers, on the 8th day of November of that year, for $825. The next lot sold was to Ulery & Zeiger, perhaps same day, for $500. The first house occupied was by Maden Brothers, who afterwards built a two story house on four-sevenths of the ground, which ground and house they recently sold for $30,000 cash. Zeiger has fine improvements on his lot and refuses to sell.

Within the two years just past, the town has enjoyed a wonderful increase in population and business, almost unprecedented in the country. At the begining of 1881 old town population was estimated at 2000 souls, all told. To-day, the begining of 1883, the whole population, (old and new town as one,) is estimated at 10,000 souls, and others coming daily, making this city their homes.

The character of the buildings is good, the most of those recently erected are of first-class brick with cut stone trimings in good taste, quite ornamental to the city. Amongst those of note is, first, the Armijo hotel, Harrison building, Cromwell block, Harsch's, Childers', First National bank, Central bank, Daily Journal, Monroe's, Baca's, Talbott's and other fine stores. The residence of Col.

Perfecto Armijo, Judge Bell's and W. Trumbull's, also the new residence of Franz Huning, Esq., which will be known as "Castle Huning." The Atlantic & Pacific railroad offices is an excellent structure. All these buildings are large, and would be first-class in any western city. Many contracts are already made for the erection of residence and business property the ensuing season, the most notable of these are the new hotel and the Armijo building of two large store rooms, second floor devoted to the use known as the Athenæum. Many of the new houses will be fine.

The hotels of the city are good and well kept, first among them, the Armijo, Rio Grande, Ballingall, Maden and Girard. A large new hotel will be completed this year for the public.

This city already enjoys many facilities for a large and important trade. This trade will be augmented with the development of her resources for business, by the construction of railroads other than those now in operation, and accommodating her enterprising population.

Her present system of railroads is as follows: The Atchison, Topeka & Santa Fe railroad extends through the territory from north to south, at El Paso connecting with the Mexican Central to Chihuahua, thence to the city of Mexico, reaching the entire Mexican system; also, the Southern Pacific and other lines entering El Paso. This company does a large business in this place, both on account of passengers and freight. The aggregate receipts at the office of this company in this city during the year ending Dec. 31, 1882, amounted to the sum of—freights, $941,046.17; tickets, $127,465.46; total, $1,068,511.63, with a constantly increasing business.

The Atlantic & Pacific railroad starts at this city and goes west to the crossing of the great Colorado river at the Needles, there connecting with that portion of the same line from San Francisco eastward, on which road passengers at this place can step on board trains and in sixty hours step aground in San Francisco, on and after next April, (said to be an assured fact). This line of road across the country is on the least dangerous ground, is located through one of the finest grazing districts on the continent, which is from the head-waters of the Rio Puerco, and the valley of the Little Colorado to its mouth, and possesses as fine natural scenery as is found anywhere in these mountainous regions. We invite special attention to the country round about San Francisco mountain ; and, especially it should be known, that this road passes within eighteen miles of the Grand Cañon, on the great Colorado river, which, to see, is worth a trip from any portion of our country ; yea, more ; the grand, the sublime sight is worth a trip from any part of the world. Nowhere else is such a sight to be seen. It is to be expressed in a simple word, as indescribable. And not least of matters in this region of interest to the traveler, are the many rich mines to be seen, and all are of importance attaching to Albuquerque.

This road, from St. Louis to San Francisco, is shorter, when finished, by 795 miles, than by way of the Southern Pacific.

Receipts of the Atlantic & Pacific railroad, at this station, for 1882, was, freight, $188,890.43 ; passenger, $17,941.15 ; total, $205,-831.58—the first regular fiscal year for this company. It is a fine showing for this station's business while the road is being built through an almost unpopulated country. This all, however, goes to show the importance of this' city and her enterprises to the whole country.

Of the roads yet uncompleted, nevertheless, sure to reach this place in the near future, is, first, the St. Louis & San Francisco, which is being vigorously pushed through the Indian Territory in this direction, so as to make an early connection at this city with the Atlantic & Pacific ; thus making, doubtless, the favorite highway across the continent ; partly on account of the mildness of the climate at all seasons of the year ; also, the safety to passengers, assured by the easy grades and gentle curves, and the security felt in avoiding the many long, high and dangerous bridges and trestles found on other roads.

Next in course is the Denver & Rio Grande, narrow gauge, which will, doubtless, soon reach this place—a very important enterprise to this whole district of our country.

The Copper City, narrow gauge, will, of necessity, be built within the lapse of a very short time, to secure to this city the minerals, stone and fine timber found contiguous to the line of this prospective railroad, and which will contribute immensely to the manufacturing and commercial advantages of this community. This road will connect with a branch of the Denver & Rio Grande from southwest Colorado, tending southeast to reach the New Mexico railway system at Albuquerque.

Another very important railroad organization has been recently accomplished, which is calculated to give this city a direct line of communication with the central south, at Napoleon, on the Mississippi river, below the mouth of the Arkansas river, by way of Little Rock west to this place. It is styled in the charter the Mississippi, Albuquerque & Inter-Ocean Railroad Company. It will be of easy construction. The propriety and utility of this enterprise should insure the speedy construction of the road from Albuquerque to Fort Smith. The eastern division is completed from Napoleon to Little Rock, and west to Fort Smith.

Next we will call attention to the contemplated narrow gauge road from this city to the White Oaks mines and mineral district, and Lincoln, the seat of justice of Lincoln county. The White Oaks mining district is reputed very rich. On this line of road are to be found large quantities of excellent timber and splendid grazing lands, with water in great plenty.

That all these lines will ultimately be a completed fact, and at an early day, admits of little doubt.

The street railroad, which is extended from the West End up Railroad avenue to First street, and south on First street to the Atlantic & Pacific shops, thence to Second street, and to the southern limits of the city, in length of line three miles, with eight cars in use, is surely of great convenience to the citizens, in their business and social relations, as it connects the extreme limits of the city by a speedy and easy means of transit. This road was built during the spring months of 1881, and the first coach was drawn over it on the 15th of May that year, it being the first street railroad built in the territory. It is a good property, the stock is not on the market for sale.

The commercial interests of the city are in a healty condition. Merchants and traders are carrying full stocks of a good class of goods, handsomely arranged in their rooms, and large amounts of all classes of merchandise, suited to the necessities of the population, are daily sold, amounting in the aggregate, during the past year, to the sum of $5,563,700—the first fiscal year for the city. Many of the large dealers have been here less than one year, who reported only for the time engaged in trade in this place. It is a good showing, considering it is only two years since it was occupied. The sales computed—goods brought here and sold, and articles of home manufacture—compare well with the trade of other cities in the country.

In this connection we will mention, in a special manner, some of the leading features of the trade :

BANKS.

There are two at present of large capital, being under the control of a high order of financial ability, and of sterling integrity. Hence it is that both the Central Bank and the First National Bank are enjoying the confidence of the people, and are reckoned first-class institutions.

MANUFACTURES.

The oldest establishment is the Glorieta flour mill, which has been in opperation several years, owned by a man of means, integrity and energy.

The Atlantic & Pacific railroad shops are large, and managed by master men, and the manipulation of skilled workmen, who receive the raw material, which they soon convert into a locomotive, passenger coach or a freight car, as may be required.

There is a foundry and machine shop, which is under judicious management and is doing a profitable business.

A plaining mill is in operation, which is doing a good business in a satisfactory manner.

A tannery is established here, and is prepared for a good, large and profitable business.

A paper mill is under construction at this place, which will, doubtless, enjoy a sure success, as such an enterprise is much needed at this point to supply the demand for that article.

Willey's flour mill was erected and put in order for business during the summer of 1880, and it has done merchant and custom work in the most satisfactory manner. The proprietor is a practical man of industry and integrity, and deserves all the good which can come to him.

A few months since some enterprising citizens organized a gas company and erected the works, by which means the city is well lighted, at reasonable rates. It is not only an important enterprise but profitable to the stock-holders.

Contractors and house builders, the head of an essential industry to the growth and prosperity of the city, and comfort of its people, are numerous, and first-class men, with ample means, combined with a cultivated taste in architecture.

There is a large quantity of Mexican filigree jewelry manufactured in this city, which is made of both gold and silver, of the most unique designs, finished in workmanlike and skillful manner, and is beautiful.

Gas fitters have a good trade and have all they can do.

Gun and lock-smiths also have a profitable employment, which seems to be satisfactory.

A matress factory is manufacturing goods in that line, and has a good business.

A candy establishment is converting a large quantity of refined sugars into pure candy, and is doing a good business to the advantage of its customers.

There are two well conducted saddle and harness establishments, which deserve a liberal patronage from the people.

A soda water manufactory is in the charge of an expenienced party upon whom the public can depend for a pure article. It is sharing a liberal support.

There are several boot and shoe shops turning out a great amount of good work, giving entire satisfaction in good fits.

There are quite a number of blacksmiths and waggon makers, and a carriage factory. All these are important industries, and are amply sustained in the community.

There are several first-class tailoring establishments, where a man in rags may enter and soon come out so metamorphosed that he has to be introduced to his wife.

The Wheelock manufactory of galvanized iron cornice, late of Las Vegas, has been removed to this city, where a great deal of beautiful work is being put up. No establishment will do more for the ornamentation of the city, and contribute much to the good taste to be shown, both in private and public buildings in times to come.

A large quantity of native wine is made in this city and vicinity of an excellent quality, as it is the pure juice of the grape. The difference in the grapes raised here produces the red, white, sweet and sour varieties of wine, all of which find a ready market, both for home consumption and shipment to distant parts of the country, where it is consumed by the people in relief of their infirmities, similar to the ailments of which Timothy was so often afflicted.

The Gran Quivera (Hubbs smelter) is an important enterprise, involving the expenditure of a large amount of money in its erection, and much more in its management, in the purchase of ore-bearing rock and the payment of the skilled hands who reduce it into a current shape. It is an enterprise of much importance to this city and surrounding country, as it will establish a home market for all the mineral-bearing rock of the hills and mountains with which our valleys are surrounded. The smelter will work gold, silver, lead and copper bearing rock, for which the best market prices are paid.

The organization known as the Albuquerque Woolen Mill Company is perfecting arrangements to commence the manufacture of cloths, flannels, janes, satinetts, shawls, blankets, yarns and other articles of woolen fabric, at an early day.

The company is composed of a number of the most enterprising and substantial men in this community, with the addition of a gentleman from a distant city, of eminently practical qualifications for the management of the large concern it will be, backed with capital sufficient to make it equal to the wants of the country.

This is already an important wool market, and with the additional demand for the factory, the quantity received here will soon run up to four or five millions of pounds annually. The establishment of these mills here will be of great importance to the wool-growing interests of the territory, as well as to this community.

A shoe and boot manufacturing establishment, in connection with the tannery, would certainly pay well if undertaken by judicious parties—because it is greatly needed.

There is organized and maintained an efficient board of trade, composed of business men. It has in the past, as it is at present, accomplishing much good for the best welfare of the people, in the promotion of all laudable enterprises.

Real estate sold in the town by real estate agents in 1882, amounts to the sum of $632,500. Amount of deferred payments on the same is $33,000, which shows a small indebtedness on so large an amount of sales.

The number of dwelling, storerooms and other buildings erected for the year ending December 31, was 450, and the cost of erecting the same was $850,000, all fully paid for, presenting a city almost entirely paid for.

The same year a bridge company was organized for the purpose of constructing a wagon bridge across the Rio Grande, which was completed at an expenditure of $22,000, which is a substantial structure of great advantage to the people residing on the west side of the river, and adds to the trade of the city.

A telephone company was formed and the apparatus with all the necessary appliances placed in working order and are now working seventy-six instruments which is of almost incalculable advantage to those who use them.

The postmaster furnished the following statement: The office was established in this place March 1881, and his receipts for the year 1882 amounted to the sum of $12,000. The estimate for the ensuing year is placed at $20,000.

This is a good place to invest money as property is still low, for a city with the advantages and prospects in the future which are clearly and distinctly defined, establishing its continued prosperity.

The mineral resources of the Sandia mountains, east a few miles, and the foot-hills within a short distance of the city, are known to be of great value by our best informed men on that subject. The various ores found and believed to abound in large quantities, are gold, silver, lead, copper and iron. The presence of each has been discovered in many localities. A great number of claims have been already located and registered, and prospectors are constantly in the mountain regions looking for the location of their future fortunes.

Copper City and many other mineral districts will contribute to the importance of this place steadily as our railroad facilities increase.

It is proper to remark that coal is also found in large quantities contiguous to this city, which is one of the sources of prosperity to all civilized communities.

On the 15th day of April, 1880, dates the advent of the first locomotive in this place, hauling a construction train. On the 22d of the same month, the first passenger coach was drawn to where the depot now stands, bearing guests to celebrate the dawning of a new era for Albuquerque and New Mexico. The most sanguine expectations of the enthusiastic men of that assemblage have been more than realized.

The supply of building material accessible to this town is abundant to assure reasonably low rates, an excellent quality of building stone, susceptible of being worked into ornamental patterns for caps, sills and posts for fronts and other uses.

An excellent quality of brick is made here, and most of the best buildings are of brick, handsomely trimmed with cut native stone.

Native timber, of good building varieties, is in great abundance, obtainable within a few miles of the city, and is sold now at reasonable prices.

Copper City and other large forests, will contribute all the timber and lumber required for this market, of the finest quality. It is also proper to remark that the expense of building here is no greater than in many eastern cities.

There is established at this place a bureau of mining and mineralogy, a miners' association for the purpose of promoting the development of that great interest in this territory. The officers are competent and urbane gentlemen. In their office they have a large stock of specimens, some of much value, and deserve an examination by the curious in such matters.

THE PRESS.

The champion of the rights and liberties of the people in the United States is creditably represented in this city in the three daily papers published here—The Journal, The Review and The Democrat. A weekly is also issued in connection with each.

The papers here have a substantial financial basis, and are fairly and ably conducted, contributing to the intelligence and energy of the people and the prosperity of the community. Their importance is fully recognized by the public.

The territorial or state fair organization has handsomely improved grounds at this place, where the annual fairs are to meet in exhibition of the products of the industry and ingenuity of the people, and the sample of ores taken from the rich mines of the country.

The cash premiums awarded at the first exhibition, held Oct. 3d to the 8th, 1881, inclusive, amounted to over $2000, exclusive of silver medals awarded on the less important exhibits. The cash premiums awarded at the second exhibition held, Sept. 18th to the 23d, 1882, amounted to over $5000, besides about $400 for silver and gold medals. Over $4000 was contributed by the citizens of Albuquerque in less than two days soliciting by the committee.

AN ANCIENT HOUSE.

A noted house in the West End, for antiquity, and for the fact that it was the home of the governor of this province, Armijo, is at this time the residence of Don Nicolas T. Armijo, vice president of the First National Bank of this city.

THE FIRST CHURCH.

The first church edifice in the territory was erected here by Gov. Uñate.   Well authenticated tradition has it that he also had made a wooden statue to the patron saint St. Francis Xavier, and presented it to the church which bore that name.   This antique piece of statuary, now not less than 335 years old, is still to be seen at the residence of a citizen of the west end, or old Albuquerque.

This church stood, and was used as such, until 1790, some 240 years, when it had so fallen into decay that it was taken down to make way for a new structure.

The new church which was erected in 1794 on the same foundations, and of the same size, form and style, is still standing and in use in the old town—both adobe buildings.   It was built by Andras Garcia, the parish priest and a Franciscan father.   The name given it is still retained, San Filipe de Neri.   So it may be said that this is practically the oldest church edifice in New Mexico, being now not less than 335 years old, and preceding the landing of the pilgrims at Plymouth Rock and the establishment of protestantism in this country by three-quarters of a century.

Within the past two years other denominations have succeeded in organizing as follows :

The Congregational church own a neat and comfortable house in which they worship, administered over by an acceptable pastor, Rev. J. M. Ashley.

The Methodist Episcopal congregation have a good house of worship, with the Rev. W. R. Kistler as pastor.

The Methodist Episcopal Church South own a neat house of worship ; pastor, Rev. W. Y. Sheppard.

The Presbyterian congregation have recently finished a brick church building, with Rev. James E. Menaul as pastor.

The Episcopal church building is of stone, and has as pastor Rev. H. Forrester.

The Roman Catholics are erecting a new church edifice of stone on the corner of Copper avenue and Sixth street, for a church—a nice structure.

SCHOOLS.

The oldest school in this community is the Catholic parochial, for the education of both sexes.   Has been in the past, as at present, of great good to the community in affording a means of education to thousands of the native population during the years gone by as well as the present time.

The Congregational and Methodist churches also have parochial schools doing all they can for the education of the youth of the city. By these schools much good is being done, but they are inadequate to the end desired, and will be until we have an organized state government under which we can have an efficient common school system with a sufficient force behind to execute the laws and enforce their observance.

The Albuquerque Academy has a new brick building well adapted for the purpose, and is in a flourishing condition, with a good corps of teachers.

The Catholics will commence early next spring the erection, in the Armijo addition, of a large and costly building, at a cost of sixty-five thousand dollars, to be used as an academy and boarding school for young ladies.

Next is the Indian school for the education of the nation's infant wards—the education of these people so long neglected by the people who were willing, until recently, to let them be Indians still.

This being a new and important matter more than ordinary attention and space will be given to its consideration.

Through the efforts of Maj. B. W. Thomas, M. D., U. S. Indian agent, the Indian office determined to establish a boarding school for the education of the Pueblo Indian youth.

The contract for conducting the school was awarded to Rev. Henry Kendall, D. D., secretary of the board of Home Missions of the Presbyterian church. On behalf of the board, in December, 1880, an adobe residence was leased of Mrs. Candelaria Garcia de Armijo, situated a short distance north of the west end. The school was organized in January, 1881, and Prof. J. S. Shearer was made superintendent.

The school was not at first popular with the Indians, and all their prejudices had to be overcome before the parents were willing to send their children to it.

The efforts of their agent and the wise conduct of the officers at the school, had the effect to steadily increase the number of pupils to fifty-seven during the spring and summer term of 1882. In July Prof. Shearer resigned and Prof. R. W. D. Bryan was appointed to succeed him.

Indian Agent Thomas visited most of the pueblos previous to the opening of the fall term, in October, 1882, found the Indians favorable to sending their children to this school, and succeeded in securing an attendance of eighty-six pupils, sixty-five boys and twenty-one girls.

Additional accommodations had to be immediately made for such an unexpected increase in numbers. Rough wooden structures were thrown up, but to make their quarters more comfortable the boys built an adobe wall on the out side, a la Indian, which makes them feel quite at home.

The following is the corps of instructors :

R. W. D. Bryan, superintendent; Miss Mariette Wood, Miss Lita A. Butler and Mrs. L. F. Tibbals, assistant teachers ; Mr. Robert Helbig, industrial teacher ; Miss M. H. Patten, matron ; Miss L. H. Patten, assistant matron ; Miss Salome Verbeck, seamstress ; Miss Clara E. Chaddock, laundress ; Mrs. Robert J. Helbig, cook.

The United States does not pay sufficiently for the labor performed and expenses necessarily incurred, consequently much of it has to be made up by the generosity of the people. This school is in good hands, and should be sustained by a philanthropic and generous public.

Nothing pleases the scholars more than to see visitors at their school, and the urbane superintendent takes great pains that his visitors receive proper attention.

SYSTEM AND NAMES OF STREETS.

Railroad avenue, the longest and principal street, extends from the eastern to the western extremity of the city, upon which the street railway is operated. We adopt it as the line between north and south. For convenience, we say North Third street and South Third street, and in like manner speak of all the streets located north and south, crossing this avenue. That portion of the city east of the Atchison, Topeka & Santa Fé railroad track is denominated "east end," and that portion of the city embraced in what was the old town is designated "west end." By this, strangers and others, will the more readily understand the immediate location of any desired place or person. It is beleived that by observing these distinctions the public convenence and interests will be subserved.

NAMES OF AVENUES NORTH OF RAILROAD AVENUE.

Copper avenue.	Perfecto avenue.
Tijeras avenue.	Mariano avenue.
Carroll avenue.	Jesus avenue.
Marquette avenue.	Castillo avenue.
Roma avenue.	Otero avenue.
Fruit avenue.	Armijo avenue.
New York avenue.	

NOTE.—Copper and Tijeras avenues extend to the extreme boundaries of the city east and west.

NAMES OF AVENUES SOUTH OF RAILROAD AVENUE.

Gold avenue.	Huning avenue.
Silver avenue.	Stover avenue.
Lead avenue.	Hazeldine avenue.
Coal avenue.	Atlantic avenue.

NOTE.—All the avenues run east and west.

NAMES OF AVENUES RUNNING PARALLEL WITH AND SOUTH OF RAILROAD AVE., AND EAST OF THE A., T. & S. F. RAILROAD TRACK.

Gold avenue,	Cromwell avenue.
Silver avenue.	Garfield avenue.
Lead avenue.	Lewis avenue.
Coal avenue.	Bell avenue.
Iron avenue.	Manuel avenue.
Highland avenue.	Trumbull avenue.
Simonds avenue.	Mass avenue.
Wheelock avenue.	Southern avenue.

NAMES OF STREETS, EAST END, CROSSING RAILROAD AVENUE, AS FOLLOWS :

Broadway street.   Water street.
Arno street.   High street.
Edith street.

NOTE.—All the streets run north and south.

NAMES OF STREETS WEST OF THE A., T. & S. F. RAILROAD TRACK, AND CROSSING RAILROAD AVE. FROM NORTH TO SOUTH, EXTREME DISTANCE OF THE CITY.

First street.   Ninth street.
Second street.   Tenth street.
Third street.   Eleventh street.
Fourth street.   Twelfth street.
Fifth street.   Thirteenth street.
Sixth street.   Fourteenth street.
Seventh street.   Fifteenth street.
Eighth street.

NOTE.—In Spanish words and names the letter J is pronounced as H.

CIVIC SOCIETIES.

MASONIC.

Temple Lodge, No. 6, A. F. & A. M.—A. M. Whitcomb, Worshipful Master; Loius Neustadt, Secretary. Stated communications first and third Thursdays of each month.

Rio Grand Chapter, No. 4, R. A. M.—Jason N. Conley, H. P.

INDEPENDENT ORDER OF ODD FELLOWS.

Maurice Trauer, N. G., Edward Strasburg, Secretary.

KNIGHTS OF PYTHIAS.

Mineral Lodge, No 4—Jesse M. Wheelock, Grand Master.

UNITED ORDER OF WORKMEN.

Edward Medler, Chief Officer.

HOSPITALS.

There is a temporary city hospital, under the care of competent persons, where the afflicted are cared for in a humane manner.

The Atlantic & Pacific Railroad Company has a well managed hospital for the protection of its employés who become sick, wounded, or in any way disabled in its service, equipped with competent nurses, cooks and steward, all in charge of competent surgeons and physicians.

MILITIA OF NEW MEXICO.

Lieut-Col. Perfecto Armijo, 2d Regt. New Mexico Militia; First Lieut. R. Q. M., Ed. W. Young, 2d Regt. New Mexico Militia.

ALBUQUERQUE GUARDS—COMPANY F., 2D REGT.

Captain, John Borradaile ; First Lieutenant, Edgar S. Howe ; Second Lieutenant, W. C. Brown. Company thirty-six men, handsomely uniformed, well drilled ; present a handsome appearance, and deport themselves like the brave men as they are. Our city should be proud of them.

OFFICIAL DIRECTORY

FEDERAL.

Tranquilino Luna, Delegate to Congress.
Lionel A. Sheldon, Governor.
William G. Ritch, Secretary.
Samuel B. Axtell, Chief Justice.
J. Bell and Warren Bristol, Associate Justices.
Henry M. Atkinson, Surveyor General.
William H. Bailhachie, Receiver of Public Moneys.
Gustavus A. Smith, United States Collector.
S. M. Barnes, United States District Attorney.
A. L. Morrison, United States Marshall.
Max Frost, Register Land Office, Santa Fe.
G. D. Bowman, Register Land Office, Mesilla.
Samuel W. Sherfey, Register Land Office, Mesilla.

TERRITORIAL.

William Breeden, Attorney General.
A. R. Owen, Attorney Second District.
S. B. Newcomb, Attorney Third District.
E. L. Bartlett, Adjutant General.
Antonio Ortiz y Salazar, Treasurer.
Trinidad Alarid, Auditor.
—— Thompson, Librarian.

COUNTY OFFICERS—BERNALILLO COUNTY.

Tomas Gutierrez, Probate Judge.
Melchior Werner, Probate Clerk and ex-officio Recorder.
Perfecto Armijo, Sheriff.
Charles W. Lewis, Treasurer.
Bernardo Valencia, First District, ⎫
José de la Luz Chavez, Second District, ⎬ County Commissioners.
Elwood Maden, Third District, ⎭
N. T. Armijo, ⎫
Ignacio Gonzales, ⎬ School Commissioners.
M. S. Otero, ⎭
José Montano Candelaria, ⎫
José Armijo y Ortiz, ⎪
Santiago L. Hubbel, ⎬ River Commissioners.
Thomas F. Phelan, ⎭
Dr. Albert E. Ealy, Coronor.

SCHEDULE OF DISTANCES FROM ALBUQUERQUE.

Going North by the Atchison, Topeka & Santa Fe Railroad.	
TO	**MILES**
Alameda..................	8
Bernalillo.................	16
Algodones................	26
Elota............	30
WALLACE.................	37
Rosaris	42
Cerrillos....	48
Ortiz.....................	56
Lamy.....................	67
SANTA FE.................	85
Manzanares........	69
Glorieta..................	77
Levy......	82
Kingman..................	86
Fulton...................	95
Pecos....................	103
Bernal...................	113
Sulzbacher...............	118
Onava....................	127
Las Vegas.................	132
Watrous..................	152
Springer........	203
Otero....................	238
Raton....	243
Trinidad.................	266
La Junta.................	348
Denver...................	472
Kansas City..............	918
St. Louis	1193
Chicago....	1407
New York....	2237

South by the same Railroad.	
Isleta......	9½
Los Lunas................	20
Belen....................	30
Sabinal...................	40
La Joya ʻʻʻ	51
Alamillo..................	62
Socorro..................	74
San Antonio..............	88
Valverde	95
San Marcial..............	102
Rincon...................	172
Las Cruces...............	205
El Paso..................	248
Nutt.....................	203
Deming..................	231
Guymas..................	650
Tucson...................	450
Yuma....................	466
Los Angeles.........	946
San Francisco............	1428

Going West by the Atlantic & Pacific Railroad.	
TO	**MILES**
Isleta....	9½
A. & P. Junction...........	12
Luna	23
Rio Puerco....	34
San José....	47
El Rito..................	59
Laguna...................	66
Cubero...................	72
McCarty's................	83
Acoma..................	88
Grants....................	96
Blue Water...............	107
Chavez...................	121
CONTINENTAL DIVIDE.... ..	130
Coolidge..................	136
Wingate..................	146
Gallup....	157
Defiance..................	165
Manuelito................	174
Allantown........	186
Sanders..................	199
Navajo Springs............	212
Billings..................	225
Carrigo..................	238
Holbrook.................	252
St. Joseph................	263
Hardy....................	275
Winslow..................	285
Dennison.............	298
Cañon Diablo....	311
Angell....................	322
Cosnino..................	333
Flagstaff (S. F. mts.)........	343
Volunteer................	355
Chalender................	367
Williams.................	377
Prescott Junction.......... ...	385
Partridge Creek...........	402
Val de Chino..............	420
Beal's Pass...............	430
Truxton Spring............	475
Peacock Spring............	494
Unalapai Valley...........	504
Wallapai Pass............. ...	513
Needles (Colo. river)........	562
Piute Pass................	606
San Diego Junction....	636
Crater Valley.............	650
Hot Springs....	705
Mojave River..............	730
Bird Point................	830
San José.................	1085
San Francisco.............	1135

STAR CLOTHING HOUSE

LEWIS & ULMAN, PROPRIETORS.

—— Dealers in Fine ——

Clothing, Furnishing Goods, Boots and Shoes, Hats and Caps

TRUNKS AND VALISES.

Sole agents for Wilson Bro's Shirts.   **ALBUQUERQUE, N. M.**

WHITE HOUSE BILLIARD PARLOR

—— THE ——

FINEST IN THE TERRITORY

Railroad Avenue.

CHAS. MONTALDO.

THOS. HAWKINS
TONSORIAL ARTIST

HAIR CUTTING A SPECIALTY.

RAILROAD AVENUE

Between First and Second Sts.

LADIES' BAZAAR

Ladies' Furnishing Goods

Millinery and Dress-Making,

PARIS & NEW YORK FASHIONS

North side R. R. Ave., bet. 2d & 3d Sts.

MRS. HEWLET & MISS CROSSON.

W. L. TRIMBLE & CO.

Livery and Transfer Company

—— * ——

FINEST TURN-OUTS IN THE CITY.

Office and Stables, North Second St., between Railroad and Copper Aves.

MARIANO ARMIJO.   ELIAS ARMIJO.   JOHN BORRADAILE.

Armijo Brothers & Borradaile

REAL ESTATE

—— AND ——

Bernalillo County Abstract Office

⊢MINES, INSURANCE AND MONEY BROKERS⊢

CONVEYANCERS AND NOTARIES.

Deeds Executed in either the English or Spanish Language

Take full Charge of Properties, Pay Taxes and Collect Rents.

MUNROE BUILDING, THIRD STREET

ALBUQUERQUE, N. M.

JOURNAL HOTEL

LAWRENCE MARRINAN, Proprietor.

RATES, $2.00 PER DAY

Corner Second Street and Silver Avenue,   - -   ALBUQUERQUE, N. M.

J. H. MOORE.   J. METZGER.

MOORE & METZGER

◄GOLD ◦ AVENUE ◦ MEAT ◦ MARKET►

Keep always on hand fresh Sausage, Head Cheese and Bologna, and all kinds of wild Game in season.

Gold Ave., between Second and Third Sts.

AUBRIGHT & WALTON

CHEMISTS AND PHARMACISTS

Dealers in Drugs and Medicines, at Wholesale and Retail.

Carry the largest and best stock in the Southwest, and respectfully solicit orders by mail or express.

Railroad Ave., between Second and Third Sts., Albuquerque, N. M.

A. J. BARR.   L. J. BARR.

BARR ❧ BARR

Attorneys at Law

Harrison Block,

ALBUQUERQUE, N. M.

J. RATEL

California Shoe Shop

FINE CUSTOM WORK

A SPECIALTY.

Railroad Ave., bet. 1st and 2d Sts.

ALBUQUERQUE DIRECTORY.

A

Aamis, William, residence west end.
Aasthr, Jbuas, residence west end.
Aascaur, Wilt, residence west end.
Abbey, W. B., boot and shoemaker, Railroad ave., bet. Second and Third sts.
Abeita, Plasido, residence west end.
Abeita, José, residence west end.
Abeita, Plasido, cook Perfecto Armijo, Tijeras st., bet. First and Second sts.
Able, D. J., cigars and tobacco, Railroad ave., between First and Second sts.
Acuma, Benido, residence west end.
Acuses, J. J., residence west end.
Adams, Andy, Ellingwood & Adams, butchers, cor. Silver ave. and south Second st., house Highland Addition.
Adams, C., machinist A. & P. round house.
Ayres, Julian, residence west end.
Agar, C. C., foreman Review Job office.
Albright, Mrs. J. G., art parlors, Gold ave., between First and Second sts.
Albright, G. F., foreman Democrat job office.
Albright, J. G., editor and manager Democrat.
Aldridge, A. C., architect A. & P. general office.
Allen, Miss Eva, boards 87 Copper ave.
Allen, Edward, moulder Albuquerque foundry.
Allison, W. H. H., agent Singer sewing machine, Masonic building, Third st.
Allyn, J. G., clerk cashier's office, A. & P. general offices.
Ahlstrom, J. H., carpenter Whitcomb & Medler, corner First st. and Gold ave.
Alsen, Andrew, boiler maker A. & P. round house.
Alexander, Barber, south Second st.
Alexander, Chas., Railroad ave., Palace saloon.
Alexander, Miss S., California suit and cloak house, Third st., bet. Railroad and Copper aves.
American Central Insurance Company, of St. Louis, Charles Etheridge, agent.
Amshon, E. C., waiter Frisco restaurant, Railroad ave., bet. Second and Third sts.
Analla, Juan, residence west end.
Analla, Antonio, residence west end.
Analla, José, residence west end.
Analla, Hector, residence west end.
Analla, Anastacio, residence west end.
Analla, Manelo, residence west end.
Anallo, Pedro, residence west end.
Anallo, Lucas, residence west end.
Analla, Anabroco, residence west end.

(29)

J. S. TORREY.   GEO. A. ANDERSON.   A. C. SLOAN.

TORREY, ANDERSON & SLOAN

(Successors to Robbins & Torrey)

——DEALERS IN——

Furniture, Queensware, Glassware, Etc.

☞ WRITE TO US FOR PRICES ☜

Undertaking Orders Promptly Attended to.

FIRST STREET.   ALBUQUERQUE, N. M

(ESTABLISHED 1881)

NICHOLS & WHITSON

Dealers in

PIANOS AND ORGANS

Musical Merchandise

Royal, St. Johns and Singer Sewing Machines

A. D. WHITSON.   Needles, Oils and Attachments for all Sewing Machines   T. E. NICHOLS.

Pianos, Organs and Sewing Machines Sold on Easy Monthly Payments,

SOUTH SECOND ST., BET. RAILROAD AND GOLD AVENUES.

THE GIRARD HOUSE

J. F. GIRARD, PROPRIETOR.

Near corner of Gold Ave. and Third St.

GOOD SAMPLE ROOMS FOR COMMERCIAL AGENTS

RATE, $2.50 PER DAY.

ALBUQUERQUE, - - - N. M.

Anderson, P. H. machinist A. & P. roundhouse.

Anderson, R. D., manager Bell Telephone Company, Railroad ave., bet. Second and Third sts.

Anderson, A., porter Santiago Baca.

Anderson, Wm., bartender, rooms Los Angeles house.

Anderson, George A., Torrey, Anderson & Sloan, furniture, First st., bet. Railroad and Gold aves.

Anderson, Charles T., cutter, J. B. Tarbox, tailor, south Second st., bet. Railroad and Gold aves.

Anderson, Frank, tailor J. B. Tarbox.

Andino, Lorenzo, residence west end.

Andrews, J. L., carpenter A. & P. yards.

Angell, B. W., division superintendent, A. & P. general offices.

Answorth, George, dishwasher Jewett house.

Ansures, Gustoral, residence west end.

Ansures, José, residence west end.

Anthony, J. D., brakeman, A. & P.

Anthony, Ordiz, clerk Lewis Bros., general merchandise, First st., bet. Railroad and Gold aves.

Apodaco, Thos., painter A. & P.

Apodaca, B., compositor Democrat office.

Apodaco, C., waiter Journal hotel, Silver ave.

Apeara, Robert, street car driver.

Apodaca, José, residence west end.

Apodaca, José 2d, residence west end.

Apodaca, Florencio, residence west end.

Apodaca, Antonio, residence west end.

Apodaca, Plasido, residence west end.

Apodaca, Catalino, residence west end.

Apodaca, Gregorio, residence west end.

Aras, Mike, waiter Girard house, cor. Third st. and Gold ave.

Aragon, Dana, residence west end.

Aragon, Miss Georgie, residence west end.

Aragon, David, residence west end.

Anchirque, José, residence west end.

Archer, Wm., carpenter, residence Highland Addition.

Archer, Wm., carpenter Whitcomb & Medler.

Archer, James, carpenter, Gold ave., bet. Second and Third sts.

Arando, Pedro, residence west end.

Arago, Antonio, wiper A. & P. roundhouse.

Armitage, W. H., draftsman Mack & Wheelock.

Armstrong, David, residence west end, vice president and superintendent Albuquerque Street Railroad Company.

Armijo Hotel, corner Railroad ave. and Third st., James G. Hope, proprietor.

Armstrong, M. A., painter, residence north Third st., between Railroad and Copper aves.

Armijo, Mariano, Armijo Brothers & Borradaile, real estate, office Monroe building, Third st.

ST. JULIEN SALOON

G. B. PINKHAM, Proprietor.

CHOICE ♦ WINES ♦ LIQUORS ♦ AND ♦ CIGARS

FINE CLUB ROOMS ATTACHED.

CORNER RAILROAD AVENUE AND SECOND STREET.

JNO. A. LEE & Co.

——Dealers in——

LUMBER { NATIVE, EASTERN AND CALIFORNIA.

Doors and Sash, Glass, Building Paper and Building Material.

FIRST STREET, ALBUQUERQUE, N. M.

MAYBEE & SCHAFFER

——DEALERS IN——

ELGIN, WALTHAM & FOREIGN WATCHES

Diamonds, Jewelry and Silverware.

The only House in Albuquerque that manufactures its own Filigree Jewelry.

Second Street, between Railroad and Gold Avenues.

Z. STAAB.   EDWARD SPITZ.   A. STAAB.

STAAB & CO.

Wholesale Dealers in

GENERAL MERCHANDISE

ALBUQUERQUE, N. M.

New York Office, 132 Church Street.

Armijo, Perfecto, sheriff Bernalillo county, house and office Tijeras st., bet. First and Second sts.

Armijo, Nicholas T., vice president First National bank.

Armijo, Elias, Armijo Brothers & Borradaile.

Armijo, Christobal, capitalist, residence west end.

Armijo, Carlos, residence west end.

Armijo, Pedro, residence west end.

Armijo, Juan Chaves, residence west end.

Armijo, Rafael, residence west end.

Armijo, Jesus, corner Sixth st. and Railroad ave., general merchandise.

Armijo, Quinno Colt, residence west end.

Armijo, Gabriel, residence west end.

Armijo, Julian, residence west end.

Armijo, Otero Francisco, real estate, residence west end.

Armijo, José Colt, residence west end.

Armijo, Romaldo, residence west end.

Ashen, John, clerk Neustadt Bros., gen'l mdse., cor. Gold ave. and First st.

Austin, Miss Eva, at Mrs. Medler's, dress maker, South Third st.

Aubright, Dr. S., physician and surgeon, Railroad ave. between Second and Third sts.

Aubright, W., Aubright & Walton, druggists, Railroad ave., between Second and Third sts.

Aubright, Harry, clerk Aubright & Walton.

B

Baca, Manuel, residence west end.

Baca, Francisco, residence west end.

Baca, Claudo, residence west end.

Baca, José, residence west end.

Baca, Birento, residence west end.

Baca, Marcus, residence west end.

Baca, Ambrocio, residence west end.

Baca, Pedro, residence west end.

Baca, Tedenco, residence west end.

Baca, Juan, residence west end.

Baca, Jesus, residence west end.

Baca, Ambrocio, residence west end.

Baca, Marcus, residence west end.

Baca, Ycidro, residence west end.

Baca, Santiago, Baca & Gray, wholesale liquor dealers, Railroad ave., bet. Second and Third sts.

Baker, C., bartender Geo. Holliday's saloon.

Baker, Robert, prop. New York Laundry, south Second st., bet. Lead and Silver aves.

Baker, Dr. C. C., physician and surgeon, south Third st., bet. Gold and Silver aves.

Bodauacco, Geo., fruits and confectionery, Railroad ave., near First st.

Balinn, F , waiter, Armijo House.

LADIES' EMPORIUM

MILLINERY ❋ DRESS-MAKING

MRS. C. L. SPOONER

PARIS, NEW YORK AND CHICAGO FASHIONS

FRENCH STAMPING DONE TO ORDER

Masonic Block, - - Albuquerque, N. M.

E. C. MONFORT

UNDERTAKER

Metallic and Wood Cloth-covered

CASES AND CASKETS

Garments, Coffins and Trimmings

Attention given to embalming and preserving bodies. Orders received for Monuments and Head stones. A full line of Show Cases on hand.

FIRST STREET, THREE DOORS FROM SILVER AVENUE

Albuquerque, N. M.

Baldridge, J. C., wholesale and retail lumber, cor. First st. and Copper ave.

Baldonado, Ujenio, residence west end.

Baldes, Manuel, residence west end.

Ball, Lyman, residence west end.

Ball, S. Y., street car driver.

Ball, Seymour, bartender, west end.

Ballissar, Padre, pastor Catholic church, west end.

Bagnall, Sam, moulder, Albuquerque Foundry & Machine Co.

Bailhache, J. M., manager Review.

Bailhache, A. L., city editor Review.

Bailhache, W H., residence west end, receiver public money, Santa Fe.

Barraclough, W. A., blacksmith, cor. Copper ave. and Third st.

Barraclough, J. T., E. J. Post & Co., hardware, Railroad ave., bet. Second and Third st.

Barraclough, H. A., E. J. Post & Co., Railroad ave.

Bush, C., wiper A. & P. round house.

Barnum, Wallace, wiper A. & P. round house.

Barrea, L. D., barber, Railroad ave.

Barrett, Wm. M., residence west end.

Barrett, S. W., residence west end.

Barnett, John, street car driver.

Barr, Leo J., Barr & Barr, att'ys at law, office cor. Railroad ave. and Second st.

Barr, A. J., Barr & Barr, att'ys at law, office cor. Railroad ave. and Second st.

Baron, Albert T., bartender.

Barrett, J., cook, Frisco restaurant.

Barta, R., blacksmith, M. Zirhut, west end.

Barnum, C., freight engineer A. & P. R. R.

Barron, Allen, night clerk Maden House.

Ballingall House, corner Lead ave. and First st.

Bartholomay, C. F., clerk, Torrey, Anderson & Sloan, furniture, First st., bet. Railroad and Gold aves.

Basye, J. W., jeweler, Railroad ave, bet. Second and Third sts.

Bayles, Chas., carpenter, residence west end.

Bell, Joseph, residence west end.

Bell, J. M., physician and surgeon and prop. American House, cor Lead ave. and Second sts.

Bell, J. W., Bell & Co., Cyclone grocery, south First st., between Gold and Silver aves.

Bearrup, John H., traveling agt. Oberne, Hosick & Co.

Beaver, Jake, mason.

Bean, Chas., Bean & Riley, bed springs manufacturers, Gold ave., near Fourth street.

Bell, M.

Bell, Joseph, judge, residence west end.

Beeks, E., carpenter, A. & P. shops.

Belford, Chas., wholesale and retail mattrass and shades, s. Third st., bet. Gold and Silver aves.

Behrens, John, grocery, west end Railroad ave.

◁RIVERSIDE ✳ HOUSE▷

One Mile South of Town

Located on the Finest Drive Out of the City.

GUS VOGHT, PROPRIETOR.

Choice Wines, Liquors and Cigars Always on Hand.

D. GOLDBERG

JEWELER & DIAMOND BROKER

——Dealer in——

Watches, Diamonds, Clocks and Filigree Jewelry

Fine Watch Repairing by Best Workmen

Opp. Opera House. ALBUQUERQUE, NEW MEXICO.

☞ Money Loaned on Jewelry ☜

Gran Quivera Mining & Smelting Company

ALBUQUERQUE, N. M.

BUYERS OF ORE AND BASE BULLION

Complete Smelting, Sampling and Assay Works

Closest Scrutiny courted and Satisfaction Guaranteed.

Correspondence Solicited. **L. C. HUBBS, Manager.**

Benson, Taylor, waiter, Rio Grande Hotel.
Benso, John H., carpenter.
Bendle, George H., foreman F. L. Pearce, wholesale lumber, Highland ad.
Bennett, Wm. H., s. Second st., near Lead ave.
Benn, Robert, butcher, cor. Silver ave. and s. Second st.
Bennett, Miss Etna, Electro Magnetic Treatment, s. First st., bet. Gold and Silver aves.
Bernal, J., laborer A. & P. shops.
Bertolone, F. Highland ad., porter Central Bank.
Berks, J. W., real estate, opposite Armijo house.
Bergere, A. M., clerk, Spiegelberg Bros., cor. First st. and Gold ave.
Berne, Chas., boiler maker, A. & P. shops
Best, C. J., fireman, A. & P. shops.
Biarasche, Geo., Maden hotel building.
Bibo, Ben, clerk, L. Kornberg, west end.
Bichard, Wm., residence west end.
Biddle, — chief clerk freight office, A. & P. railroad.
Biggens, Thos., blacksmith A. & P. shops.
Bistaf, John, residence west end.
Bibikov, N. A., mining bureau, Third st. between Gold and Railroad aves.
Blanchard, James, plumber Vose & Co., First st. between Gold and Silver aves.
Black, Wm., foreman blacksmith A. & P. shops.
Blerch, John, butcher, Gold ave.
Block, J. B., teamster, in Frank Armijo addition.
Blomberg, Chas., cook Frisco restaurant, Railroad ave.
Blondin, R. J., cook Murphy lodging house, First st. between Railroad and Copper aves.
Boatright, D., foreman painters A. & P. shops.
Bodnell, J., carpenter A. & P. shops.
Bodnell, J. F., blacksmith A. & P. shops.
Boerstler, Geo., painter, Silver ave., between Second and Third sts.
Bogart, James, shipping clerk Stover, Crary & Co.
Bohn, John, Copper ave., between Sixth and Seventh sts.
Bolthinghouse, F. J., conductor A. & P. railroad.
Boles, N. A., assayer Gran Quivera smelter, one mile south of city.
Bolton, Thos., plumber Pegram & Cline.
Bowman, G. C., carpenter A. & P. shops.
Bonnell, J. E., carpenter A. & P. shops.
Bonsall, C. E., residence west end.
Borchert, Wm., Scott & Borchert, wholesale furniture and carpets, First st., between Gold and Silver aves.
Bordan, Wm., residence west end.
Borradaile, Capt. John, Armijo Bros. & Borradaile, real estate, Monroe building, Third st.
Boston, C., blacksmith A. & P. shops.
Bowen, F., carpenter, corner First st. and Silver ave.
Bowen, Wilbert, fruit and news stand, Railroad ave. near First st.

| MAINZ a RHEIN | GEISENHEIM a R. | LEADVILLE | GUNNISON CITY |
| Germany | Germany. | Colo | Colorado. |

⤜ C. CONRAD & CO ⤛

WHOLESALE

LIQUOR ✳ DEALERS

Main Offices, Nos. 411 to 419 North Sixth St.

St. Louis, Mo.

PROPRIETORS

Conrad's Original Budweiser Beer,

Conrad's "Moss Rose" Bourbon,

Conrad's "Governor's Choice" Rye

Conrad's Rhine Wines & Clarets

Importers and Jobbers in all known Brands of

⤜WINES, ✢ CHAMPAGNES, ✢ COGNACS⤛

And Liquors in General.

| DENVER, COLO, | DALLAS, TEXAS, | BUENA VISTA, COLO. |

Bowen, E. W., clerk fruit and news stand, Railroad ave. near First st.

Bowlby, Wm., freight engineer A. & P. railroad.

Bonie, Robt., clerk Wells, Fargo Express Company.

Boyd, Andy, engineer A., T. & S. F. railroad.

Boyle, John, saloon, Railroad ave., between Second and Third sts.

Boyd, Chas., Boyd & Wade, proprietors opera house.

Brady, John, Lock & Brady, proprietor Oasis saloon, Railroad ave., between Second and Third sts.

Brady, John, residence west end.

Brady, Wm. W., residence west end.

Bradley, A. L., Bradley & Macbeths, dentists.

Brand, Frank, leader of orchestra opera house, Railroad ave., bet. Gold and Railroad aves.

Bram, David, residence west end.

Bram, John H., residence west end.

Brehan, John, boiler washer A. & P. shops.

Brennon, Joseph, carpenter A. & P. shops.

Brennon, Jake, policeman.

Brennon, Robt., plasterer, Highland addition.

Brewster, R. S., carpenter E. Nichols.

Briggs, A. C., clerk chief engineer's office, A. & P. railroad.

Briggs, J. M., painter, Highland addition.

Brickner, W. F., carpenter A. & P. shops.

Brock, E. A., contractor and builder, Highland addition.

Brock, Arthur, carpenter, corner Second st. and Copper ave.

Brooks, C. H., South Fourth st., bet. Gold and Railroad aves.

Brownwell, J. S., wholesale lumber, coal and paints, corner Lead avenue and First st.

Brown, O. M., machinist A. & P. round house.

Brown, John, machinist A. & P. round house.

Brown, O., Brown & Lawson, Santa Fe lunch counter.

Brown, O. S., freight clerk A., T. & S. F. railroad office.

Brown, R. P., passenger conductor A. & P. railroad.

Brown, Simon, bakery First st., between Gold and Silver aves.

Brown, Bill, baber, center of plaza, west end.

Brown, Wm., mason.

Bryan, Prof. R. W. D., superintendent Indian school.

Bryan, R. T., Maden hotel barber shop.

Bucklin, D. S., carpenter A. & P. shops.

Bunlel, William, carpenter, corner First st. and Silver ave.

Bunnell, M., day editor Journal.

Burris, John, blacksmith A. & P. shops.

Burris, Harry, clerk New Mexico News Co., at post office.

Burton, George, cook Jewett house.

Burdock, Frank, cook Rio Grande house.

Burris, F. H., proprietor Rio Grande hotel.

Burke, Wallace, Pacific Coal Co., First st., between Railroad and Gold aves.

Burke, James, contractor, boards at Armijo house.

CHAS. ✴ ETHERIDGE

Notary Public

OFFICE
OVER CENTRAL BANK   ALBUQUERQUE

—— DEALS IN ——

INSURANCE—IN—ALL FORMS

Representing a large line of the best companies, including

Mutual Life Insurance Co., New York.
Travelers Life and Accident, Hartford, Conn.
Liverpool, London & Globe Insurance Co.
Commercial Union, London.
Insurance Co. of North Americo, Philadelphia
Springfield Fire and Marine, Springfield, Mass.
Pennsylvania Fire Insurance Co., Philadelphia.
German-American Insurance Co., New York.
Scottish Union and National, Z. B.
Western Assurance Co., Toronto, Canada.
Home Insurance Company, New York.
Phœnix Insurance Office, London.
American Central Insurance Co., of St. Louis, Mo.
London Assurance Company, London.

REAL ESTATE

Bargains for Investors, whether to locate for Business, Residence or for Profit.

☞ My List is open at all times to the anxious enquirer, and I take pleasure in showing properties for sale. Correspondence solicited.

Burke, John, contractor, boards at Armijo house.
Burke, Wm H., proprietor Ballingall hotel.
Burke, W. S., editor Journal.
Burke, W. D., saloon, Railroad ave., near First st.
Butler, L. M., Fuller & Butler, Frisco restaurant, Railroad ave., bet. Second and Third sts.
Burr, S. M., residence west end.
Bullock, E., manager New Mexico News Co., at post office.
Busse, Paul, clerk county clerk's office.
Byron, Galen, compositor Review.

C

Cassady, George, mason.
Cano, Pinfilo, laborer west end.
Card, J. B., messenger Wells Fargo Express Company
Carter, E., waiter Armijo house.
Carnilaz, Angel, harness maker, Railroad ave., bet. Third and Fourth sts.
Caldwell, Thomas, carpenter Whicomb & Medler.
Caldwell, John, carpenter Whitcomb & Medler.
Carl, E., Carl & Thompson, grocers, South Third st.
Carmile, W. A., painter, Silver ave., bet. Second and Third sts.
Capron, Ed., Los Angeles lodging house.
Carter, W. P., photographer, corner Lead ave. and First st.
Carro, M., laborer A. & P. shops.
Carpenter, John, Carpenter & Swygart, painters, Second st., between Railroad and Copper aves
Catron, Thomas, attorney at law, corner of Gold ave. and First st.
Carter, Allen, waiter Rio Grande hotel.
Carabajal, Bibian, residence west end.
Carabajal, P., residence west end.
Carabajal, Solomon, residence west end.
Candelaria, Jesus, residence west end.
Candelaria, José, residence west end.
Candelaria, Teofeli, residence west end.
Candelaria, Antonio, residence west end.
Candelaria, Manuel, residence west end.
Candelaria, Balino, residence west end.
Candelaria, Juan Antonio, residence west end.
Candelaria, Ygnacio, residence west end.
Candelaria, Benito, residence west end.
Candelaria, Apodaca, residence west end.
Canning, Wm., machinist A. & P. shops.
Canadolris, C., laborer, A. & P. shops.
Cardale, A., city livery stables, Fourth st., bet. Railroad and Copper aves.
Chandler, José, fireman Albuquerque Gas Co.
Chaves, J., proprietor St. Julien restaurant.
Cadden, A. M., residence west end.
Caddagan, G. W., constable precinct No. 12.

◄HONEST AND FEARLESS►

The Evening Review

LARGEST CIRCULATION OF ANY PAPER IN NEW MEXICO.

Daily, $10.00.   Weekly, $3.00.

NO NEWS ESCAPES US.

Fine Job and Book Printing a Specialty.

Office in Review Building, }   **BAILHACHE & CO., Prop's**
Gold Avenue.   }   Albuquerque, N. M.

RELIABLE AND STANDARD

CIGARETTES

◄◄◄ ►•AND•◄ ►►►

►►TOBACCO◄◄

Manufactured by

►WM. S. KIMBALL & CO.◄

*The Connoisseurs and Pioneers of
America in Fine Goods.
Twelve First Prize Medals.*

Fragrant Vanity,
New Vanity Fair,
Three Kings

Peerles Tobacco Works.   Sold in all Parts of the World.

Campbell, Robt., blacksmith A. & P. round house.
Cedillo, Pedro, wiper A. & P. shops.
Cedillo, R., laborer A. & P. shops.
Cedillo, F., wiper A. & P. shops.
Chalender, Geo. F., superintendent motive power and machinery A. & P. R. R.
Chambers, W., boards at Armijo house.
Charlie, W. A., Alameda ave., near South Fifth st.
Chaves, M., laborer A. & P. shops
Chaves, C., residence west end.
Christan, Maquer, residence west end.
Chaves, José M., residence west end.
Chaves, Rafael, residence west end.
Chaves, Greseno, residence west end
Chaves, Elias, residence west end.
Chaves, Julian, residence west end.
Chaves, Meliton, residence west end.
Chavez, Aldios, compositor Democrat.
Champion, J. W., plumber Vose & Co.
Childers, W. B., attorney at law, Gold ave., bet. First and Second sts.
Chung, Lee, Chinese bazar, oppposite Armijo hotel.
Christian, O. C., architect and superintendent, Lewis building, First st.
Clark, Charles, bartender St. Julian saloon.
Clark, E. S., clerk Stover, Crary & Co.
Cleland, A. W., book-keeper Ilfeld & Co.
Collings, P. E., commission merchant, cor. First st. and Gold ave.
Cleto, Pedro.
Clomumbia, Morris, mechanic New Mexico Novelty Works.
Clapp, John, foreman tinsmiths A. & P. shops.
Clousen, H., clerk Exchange hotel, west end.
Clark, John, laborer west end.
Clark, J. R., compositor Democrat.
Clark, J. C., carpenter, corner Second st. and Copper ave.
Crosta, Ed., tinner, Stein, Mandell & Co.
Creamer, José, residence west end.
Cromwell, O. E., pres't Albuquerque Street Railroad Co., residence west end.
Crane, F. E., surveyor W. F. Crane.
Crane, Wm. F., Real Estate and Insurance, South First st., between Gold and Silver aves., house South Union st., bet. Gold and Silver aves.
Crary, George F., Stover, Crary & Co., wholesale groceries, corner First st. and Railroad ave.
Craft, Wm., residence Frank Armijo Addition.
Carr, Joseph, clerk Scott & Bochert.
Crammer, C., fireman A. & P. railroad.
Crocker, F. M., clerk cashier's office A. & P. railroad.
Cross, F. H., brakeman A. & P. railroad.
Crosby, Walter, waiter Oriental restaurant.
Crossan, Miss Mary, Hewlet & Crossan, millinery, Railroad ave., bet. Second and Third sts.

EDMOND NICHOLS

⇀ Contractor × and × Builder ↼

Estimates Furnished on all Kinds of Work

CORNER SILVER AVENUE and FIRST STREET

Albuquerque, N. M.

REAL ESTATE	LAND IN BLOCKS
Bought, sold and managed. Houses, rooms and ranches rented. Rents collected. Taxes paid. Estates managed.	And ranches in Texas, New Mexico, Arizona, California and Mexico; also Spanish and Mexican land grants of all dimensions.

| JOHN W. BERKS
Of Philadelphia, Pa.

W. A. FAIRFIELD
Of Golden, Colo.

Established, 1881

At present location. | **BERKS & FAIRFIELD**
MINES AND LAND
Negotiators, Promoters, Assayers, Metalurgists Mining Engineers and Managers. More than thirty years of successful business experience.
ALBUQUERQUE, N. M. | MONEY LOANED
On real estate and personal property.

Commercial Paper
Negotiated.

Collections Made |

MEXICO MINING BUREAU

We furnish reliable data, when obtainable, respecting mines and mining districts, for the advisement of investors and engineers; such information compremends location, improvements, title, yield, present value and probable increase, etc.; also advise as to kind and extent of machinery for mining and reduction works, with estimate of cost; and furnish directions for opening and working mining property.

ASSAY OFFICE	Mines and Prospects
And Chemical Laboratory. Samples by mail will receive prompt and careful attention. Four ounces are sufficient. Send for terms for assaying.	We buy, sell, bond, stock and report on mining property ; also, undertake the suspension of mining and of developing work on new property.

Crossan, E., A. & P. coal office, First st., near A. & P. shops.
Crooks, A. B., blacksmith A. & P. shops.
Capell, R. C., agent C. O. D. clothing house, Chicago, boards at Armijo house.
Cundiff, Miss Julia, dressmaker, Second st., bet. Lead and Silver aves.
Custers, M., Frank & Custers, Third st., bet. Railroad and Gold aves
Cottrell, Joe., book-keeper, opera house.
Commercial Union Fire Insurance Company of London, Chas. Etheridge, agent.
Cook, J., clerk E. J. Post & Co., hardware, Railroad ave.
Cook, Wm., machinist, A. & P. shops
Conner, Albert, proprietor Marble Hall, Railroad ave., bet. Second and Third sts.
Contreras, Antonio, residence west end.
Conway, M. E., machinist A. & P. shops.
Contreras, Pedro, residence west end.
Cohn, I., proprietor Great Western hotel, First st., bet. Gold and Silver aves.
Coddington, A. W., Jones & Coddington, Albuquerque Dairy, two miles north of town.
Codington, Ed., clerk E. S. Codington & Co.
Codington, A. M., commission merchant, cor. Gold ave. and First st.
Codington, E. S., furniture, Gold ave., bet. First and Second sts.
Codington, W., furniture, Gold ave., bet. First and Second sts.
Cook, J. M., carpenter A. & P. shops.
Conley, J. A., carpenter A. & P. shops.
Condalario, J., laborer A. & P. shops
Condalario, L., laborer A. & P. shops.
Conley, C. E., residence west end.
Copeland, A.. Highland addition.
Cook, E. L., stationer A. & P. R. R.
Costello, Frank, boards at Journal hotel.
Condiff, Geo., bartender Journal hotel.
Coon, H. W., bartender, Geo. Holloday's, First st.
Coalson, E. B., helper A. & P. shops.
Cowan, C. P., messenger Wells, Fargo Express Company.
Cobb, D. W., agent Wells, Fargo Express Company.
Corbin, W. L., collector Central bank.
Cox, Sam., porter Stein, Mandell & Co.
Conroy, Robt., clerk Stein, Mandell & Co.
Conley, Dr. J. N., physician and surgeon, office with Conley & Walton.
Connelly, Wm., blacksmith A. & P. shops.
Cooper, Miss, room 4, McKinney building.
Conlim, W. E., barber, Armijo hotel.
Cushing, E. G., waiter, Frisco restaurant.

D

Davidson, John, blacksmith A. & P. shops.
Daley, F. M., operator A. & P. railroad.
Damon, L. E., chief clerk A., T. & S. F. railroad office.
Daunenbaum, Max, clerk, Ilfeld & Co., general merchandise.

J. E. SAINT & CO

Albuquerque, N. M.

Wholesale and Retail

Groceries and Queensware

BAR FIXTURES, CHANDELIERS, LAMPS, and

STRATTON ⹋ & ⹋ STORM'S ⹋ CIGARS

A SPECIALTY

Mountaineer ⹋ Billiard ⹋ Hall

ALBUQUERQUE, N. M.

→ Cards, Poker Chips, Sporting Goods ←

WINES, LIQUORS & CIGARS

Railroad Avenue,
Bet. First & Second Sts. } **PETERSON & McKEE, Proprietors.**

Damlon, Michael, residence west end.
Davis, L. E., printer, Journal office.
Davis, L., bartender, Marble Hall.
Daniels, Dare, stock ranch four miles south of town.
Dayton, F., carpenter A. & P. shops.
Deacy, W. H., laborer A., T. & S. F. railroad.
Demais, Joe., soda manufacturer, Frank Armijo addition.
Deering, Walter, clerk, Putney & Trask.
Deeris, Geo., mason, residence Highland addition.
Delehanty, Thos., car repairer A. & P. shops.
DeMares, José, residence west end.
Denser, Miss Maggie, boards at Vine Cottage.
Dennison, W. C., cashier A. & P. railroad.
Dickman, Alio, residence west end.
Dinan, M. R., residence Frank Armijo addition.
Dinnick, Frank, brakeman A., T. & S. F. railroad
Dix, A. F., teamster Highland addition.
Diaz, Al., California harness shop, Railroad ave., bet Third and Fourth sts.
Dickman, Otto, clerk F. Huning, west end.
Dillmann, C., blacksmith A. & P. shops.
Dominquez, Santos, county jailer, west end.
Dominquez, Cornelio, deputy sheriff, west end.
Dominquez, José, shoemaker, west end.
Dominquez, Jr., west end.
Dobson, M. D., Dobson & Pratt, groceries, Highland addition.
Donahue, John, blacksmith and wagon maker, cor. Copper ave. and Third st.
Douglas, Thos. G., attorney at law, Lewis' building, up stairs.
Donahue, Wm., mason, west end.
Donaven, James.
Dold, Henry, Dold & Hostetter, general merchandise, Gold ave., bet. First and Second sts.
Dunica, L., book-keeper, Stein, Mandell & Co., hardware.
Dounce, J. W., residence Frank Armijo addition.
Donnelly, F., blacksmith A. & P. shops.
Donnelly, J. W., contractor and builder, Highland addition.
Donnelly, W· W., carpenter, J. W. Donnelly, Highland addition.
Donnelly, James, yard master A., T. & S. F. railroad.
Drury, J. W., general fireman A. & P. carpenter department.
Drury, J. H., master carpenter A. & P. yards.
Drury, A. J., carpenter A. & P. shops.
Draper, E. A., harness maker, north Second st.
Duran, José, residence west end.
Duran, Juan, residence west end.
Duran, Bisente, residence west end.
Duran, Lusiano, residence west end.
Duran, Juan R., residence west end.
Duran, Manuel, residence west end.
Duran, Francisco, residence west end.

Duran, Martin, residence west end.
Duran, José J., residence west end.
Duran, José A , residence west end .
Duran. Pedro, residence west end .
Duran, Mariano, residence west end.
Duran, Nirques, residence west end .
Duffy, J., nurse A. & P. hospital.
Dunbar, E. H , collector Journal office.
Duchesneau, A., mechanic, Mew Mexico Novelty Works.
Dugan, J. H., cor. Lead ave. and south Second st .
Dunham, J. N., book-keeper, Bell & Co.
Dun, Dr., hospital stewart, A. & P, hospital.
Dohl, Albert, machinist, A. & P. yards.

E

Ealy, Dr. Albert E., physician and surgeon, Gold avenue, bet. First and Second sts.
Eagen, Thos., car repairer.
Easterday, Dr. G. S., physician and surgeon, Third st., between Railroad and Gold aves.
Easton, Frank, restaurant.
Eberhardt, Louis, saloon, near A. & P. shops.
Eckel, Geo. C., Van Slyck & Rhinehart, general merchandise.
Edie, V. P., manager Oberne. Hosick & Co., hides, office cor. south First st. and Silver ave.
Eishom, Chris., machinist, A. & P. yards.
Eibel, Gus., blacksmith, Copper ave.
Elliott, Henry, wholesale flour and feed, Railroad ave., opp. Armijo house.
Elton, Wm., fireman A & P. yards.
Ellingwood, G. W., Ellingwood & Adams, meat market, cor. south Second st. and Silver ave.
Emftage, Henry, boards at Journal hotel.
Emmert, David B., real estate and insurance. Third st., bet. Railroad and Gold aves.
Eronto, José, residence west end.
Eronto, Julian, residence west end.
Erickson, John, wiper A. & P. shops.
Erickson, —, helper A. & P. yards.
Erbeck, Con., clerk, Chas. Walthers, south Third st., bet. Gold and Silver aves.
Etheridge, Chas, real estate and insurance, and notary public, over Central bank.
Evans, James, pressman, Journal office.
Evans, Harry, laborer, section house, Highland addition.
Everts, Frank, bartender.

F

Farnsworth, J. W., freight clerk, A., T. & S. F. railroad office.
Fairfield, W. A., Berks & Fairfield, real estate and mines, Railroad ave., opp. Armijo house.

M. WERNER

Probate Clerk and Notary Public

MAIN STREET. - - - WEST END

———•———

LEGAL PAPERS DRAWN

—AND—

ESTATES SETTLED

⤜St. Julien's Restaurant⤛

EUGENE VARCHE & J. CHAVES

PROPRIETORS

———

OYSTERS IN EVERY STYLE

All kinds of Wild Game in Season.

N. side Railroad Ave., bet. Second and Third Sts.

ALBUQUERQUE, N. M.

Favor, F. C., auction and commission, Railroad ave., bet. First and Second sts.

Falk, J. A., cook, A. & P. hospital.

Fede, Tathee, pastor, cathedral, west end.

Fisher, W., proprietor Exchange hotel, west end.

Finley, Henry, carpenter, E. Nichols, cor. First st. and Silver ave.

Finnegan, J., hostler, J. W. Kennedy, First st., bet. Railroad and Copper aves.

Fisher, J. W., carpenter, Whitcomb & Medler.

Fisler, A. José, residence west end.

Fish, E., freight conductor A., T. & S F. railroad.

Flornoy, M. W., teller Central bank.

Flinn, S., Maden hotel barber shop.

Flersheim, J., traveling salesman Ilfeld & Co.

Foster, Jas. T., clerk engineer's office, A. & P. railroad.

Fountain, A., residence west end.

Foote, Irving, tinner, Vose & Co.

Furce, Miss Grace, at Vine Cottage.

Fox, R. P., Fox & Rutherford, carpenters, Highland addition.

Ford, Miss Hattie, proprietress Alameda house, Second st., bet. Railroad and Copper aves. Neatly furnished rooms.

Forrester, Henry, residence west end.

Frank & Custers, wholesale paper, south Third st., bet. Railroad and Gold aves.

Frisell, J. H., machinist, A. & P. round house.

Frost, Geo., conductor A. & P. railroad, residence south Fourth st.

French, F. F., carpenter A. & P. shops.

Fritch, F. A., real estate and insurance.

Francisco, Miss Maud, Copper ave.

Franco, Frank, proprietor restaurant, cor. Second st. and Gold ave.

Fuller, J. W., boards at Armijo hotel.

Frizell, Wm., carpenter, A. & P. yards.

Fulthey, C. E., engineer plaining mill, A. & P. yards.

Fuller, A. K., Fuller & Butler, Frisco restaurant, Railroad ave., bet. Second and Third sts.

G

Galaway, J., contractor and builder, north Sixth st., between Railroad and Copper aves.

Gallager, J., nurse, A. & P. hospital.

Gallego, Juan, residence west end.

Galaway, J., Galaway & Smith, contractors and builders, office cor. Third st. and Copper ave.

Gamble, D., carpenter, E. Nichols, cor. First st. and Silver ave.

Garcia, M., gardener, Copper ave., bet. Sixth and Seventh sts.

Gacia, J, gardner, Copper ave., bet. Sixth and Seventh sts.

Garcia, Salbado, residence west end.

Garcia, M., residence west end

Garcia, Ycido, residence west end.

Garcia, Juan, residence west end.

PERFECTO + ARMIJO + & + BROTHER'S

ADDITION

CHEAP BUILDING LOTS

◄GUARANTEED DEEDS GIVEN►

Chance to Procure Pleasant Homes

——— IN THE ———

◄MOST DESIRABLE PART OF THE CITY►

——— ON ———

Easier Terms than any Real Estate firm can Offer

THE PERFECTO ARMIJO & BRO'S ADDITION TO ALBUQUERQUE

has just been laid off and surveyed, and five hundred of the most favorably situated lots in the city are placed upon the market. This addition is just north of Tijeras Cañon street and between Fourth and Eighth streets. It presents these advantages to investors:

The lots are higher and consequently more healthful than those in other parts of the city.

They are convenient to the business portion of New Albuquerque and within a minute's walk of the street cars.

Acequias with running water surround them, furnishing a continual and pure water supply for household and gardening purposes.

Being the sole owners of this addition, our prices are without commissions and are consequently lower than those of any real estate agency in Albuquerque. This is a chance for those of limited means to secure homes at small cost.

For terms apply to the office of

PERFECTO ARMIJO, OR ARMIJO BROTHERS & BORRADAILE.

Garcia, Josey A., residence west end.
Garcia, Manuel, residence west end.
Garcia, José Y., residence west end.
Garcia, Amado, residence west end.
Garcia, Pacheco, residence west end.
Garcia, Ambroca, residence west end.
Garcia, Antonio, residence west end.
Garcia, José A., residence west end.
Garcia, Candelaria, residence west end.
Garcia, Francisco, residence west end.
Garcia, Pedro, residence west end.
Garcia, José Y. A., residence west end.
Garcia, Candedo, residence west end.
Garcia, Diego, 2d, residence west end.
Garcia, Rafael, residence west end.
Girard House, cor. Gold ave. and Third st.
Garcia, Pedro A, residence west end.
Garrett, F J., brakeman, A & P. railroad.
Gasd, Frank, clerk, Hyman & Co.
Gabaldon, Rafael, residence west end.
Gabaldon, Juan Esteban, residence west end.
Gataldon, Juan, residence west end.
Gataldon, Francisco, residence west end.
Geary, Daniel, cashier First National bank.
German-American Fire Insurance Co., of New York, Chas. Etheridge, agent.
Gephart, H. C., commission, opp. Armijo house.
Gee, Lee, south Second st., bet. Silver and Lead aves.
Gilbert, G. H., messenger Wells, Fargo & Co. Express.
Gilles, L. P., Gardner & Gilles, New York clothing house.
Giddings, E., carpenter, A. & P. shops.
Girard, Peter, clerk Girard house.
Girard, J. F., proprietor Girard house, cor. Third st. and Gold ave.
Gilley, Frank, porter, T. Romero & Son, general merchandise.
Goff, James, blacksmith A. & P. shops.
Gonzales, Adelaido, manager T. Romero & Son, west end.
Gonzales, Cris, residence west end.
Gonzales, Mariano, residence west end.
Gordon, Dr. E. A., physician and surgeon, Third st., between Railroad and Copper aves.
Goodale, S. N, insurance agent, Third st., bet. Gold and Silver aves.
Gooh, George, residenc west end.
Goodman, J., painter, Silver ave., bet. Second and Third sts.
Goodman, Herman C., Rosenwald Bros., cor. Railroad ave. and Third st.
Goldstein, Joseph, Goldstein & Pechner, Boston clothing house
Goldberg, D., jeweler, Railroad ave., opp. opera house.
Goldberg, L. C., clerk, D. Goldberg.
Gotlief, L., clothing, corner Second st. and Railroad ave.
Grunsfeld, A., manager Speigleberg Bros., general merchandise.

Henry Dold.   **Louis Hostetter.**

DOLD & HOSTETTER

(Successors to T. Romero & Son)

——Wholesale and Retail Dealers in——

GENERAL MERCHANDISE

Gold Ave., bet. 1st and 2d Sts.

☞ Orders Filled and Sent to any Part of the Territory.

T. H. KENNEDY

Transfer, Sale and Livery Stables

ALBUQUERQUE, N. M.

First Street, between Railroad and Copper Aves.

FIRST-CLASS TURNOUTS AND RELIABLE TEAMS

Always on hand.

Grunsfeld, A. A., clerk, Speigleberg Bros., general merchandise.
Greb, John G., carpenter, Whitcomb & Medler.
Green, W. C., book-keeper, Chas. Etheridge.
Green, Lew, bartender, bet. Railroad and Copper aves.
Green, Thomas, mason, Highland addition.
Greenleaf, J. M., conductor A. & P. railroad.
Greenleaf, M., house on Silver ave., bet. First and Second sts.
Greigo, Julian, residence west end.
Greigo, Pablo, residence west end.
Griffen, Thomas, brakeman, A. & P. railroad.
Graves, —, proprietor Rio Grande hotel, cor. Lead ave. and Second st.
Graham, F., painter, A. & P. shops.
Grant, A. A., railroad contractor, house on Tijeras and Fifth sts.
Greening, M., clerk, Railroad ave., bet. Third and Fourth sts.
Gretz, F., baker, corner Silver ave. and First st.
Gray, Capt., Baca & Gray, wholesale liquors, Railroad ave.
Guiterrez, George, groom, Perfecto Armijo.
Geissner, George, day clerk, Rio Grande hotel.
Gutienes, José, residence west end.
Gutienes, Mariano, residence west end.
Gutienes, Juan, residence west end.
Gutienes, José, Jr., grocer, residence west end.
Gutienes, George, residence west end.
Gutienes, Juan, 2d, residence west end.
Gutienes, Domingo, residence west end.
Grey, Herbert, machinist, A. & P. shops.
Gundell, J. C., draftsman, A. & P. offices.

H

Hazeldine, W. C. lawyer, west end.
Hall, C., waiter, Armijo hotel.
Hall, Dr. W., physician and surgeon, Highland addition.
Hall, A. P., bill clerk, A., T. & S. F. office.
Halmer, Otto, baker, First st., bet. Railroad and Copper aves.
Harsch, A., bakery and fancy groceries, First st., bet. Gold and Silver aves.
Hardt, Charles L., laundry, east of A. & P. shops.
Hardy, D., superintendent of telegraph, A. & P. railroad.
Harlow, M. W., Highland addition.
Hart, Fred., wiper, A. & P. yards.
Hatch, J. P., brass-moulder, Albuquerque Foundry & Machine Co.
Hatcher, H. G., porter, Armijo hotel.
Harris, H. V., clerk, T. Romero & Son.
Harris, D., porter, Armijo hotel.
Harris, F. W., draftsman, A. & P. general office.
Harris, Henry, residence west end.
Harris, Henry, leader of band, opera house.
Hamlin, Arthur, manager Railroad News Co., north Third st.
Hamble, M. P., conductor, A. & P. railroad, residence south Seoond st.

Chas. Boyd.   Tom Wade.

BOYD & WADE

OPERA HOUSE

ALBUQUERQUE, N. M

OPEN EVERY NIGHT

A Fine Entertainment embracing

VAUDEVILLE, VARIETY AND BURLESQUE

BOYD & WADE, Managers and Proprietors.

ARMIJO HOUSE

Albuquerque, N. M.

JAS. G. HOPE, - PROPRIETOR

The Only First Class Hotel in the City.

Harman, F., tinsmith, A. & P. shops.

Handley, G. W., manager I. X. L. laundry, corner Lead ave. and First st.

Hansen, Charles, mason.

Hanson, M., nurse, A. & P. hospital.

Hanlon, John, blacksmith, A. & P. shops.

Hany, George Y., foreman tin shop, A. & P.

Hawkins, D. C., porter, J. E. Saint & Co.

Hawkins, Thomas, proprietor barber shop, Railroad ave., between First and Second sts.

Harward, W. T., night watchman, A. & P. railroad.

Hawley, C. B., Stover, Crary & Co.

Hawley, P. J., post office fruit stand.

Haynes, C. W., second hand store, south First st.

Hazlett, J., fireman, A. & P. railroad.

Headen, Richard, residence west end.

Heacock, W. C., night editor Journal.

Hedden, E. S., conductor, A. & P. railroad.

Hegman, Charles, carpenter, corner Copper avenue and Fourth st.

Heiser, Dick, bartender, corner Third st. and Gold ave.

Helbig, Miss R., cook, Albuquerque Indian school.

Helbig, Robert, industrial teacher, Indian school.

Helling, F., clerk, Tarlina's, general merchandise, Gold ave.

Herman, A. F., residence west end.

Herman, —, carpenter, north Second st., between Railroad and Copper aves.

Henig, Robert, carpenter, A. & P. shops.

Henig, Henry, carpenter, A. & P. shops.

Henry, Will A., music teacher, Highland addition.

Hessins, J. H., blacksmith, A. & P. shops

Hewlett, Miss Lucy, Hewlett & Crossan, millinery, Railroad ave., bet. Second Third sts.

Highwarden, B. W., barber, south Second st.

Hinton, M. J., portrait painter, Gold ave., bet. First and Second sts.

Hilton, Archie, marshal, west end.

Hitchcock, Charles, carpenter, Whitcomb & Medler.

Hill, John A., residence west end.

Hills, L. H., jeweler, Maybe & Schaffer.

Hobac, T. N., watchmaker.

Hobsin, J. G., bartender, Charles Zeiger.

Hobbs, M., carpenter, A. & P. shops.

Hobbs, A. B., warehouseman, A., T. & S. F. railroad.

Hoffeman, C., musician, opera house.

Hogan, Michael, saloon, corner First st. and Lead ave.

Hogland, Ed., engineer, corner Ninth st. and Lead ave.

Holladay, Geo., prop'r George's Place, First st., between Railroad and Gold aves.

Holdoway, Mrs. M., groceries, etc., First st., bet. Gold and Silver aves.

Hostetter, Louis, Dold & Hostetter, general merchandise, Gold ave., between First and Second sts.

The Morning Journal

Published Daily and Weekly

BY THE ALBUQUERQUE PUBLISHING COMPANY

THE JOURNAL IS

The Popular Paper of Albuquerque

AND THE SUNDAY EDITION IS THE

Most Widely Circulated Journal in the Territory

The Daily Circulates among all classes of people; it reaches more effective-
ly than any other journal the traveling public and the interior
merchants, and also all those interested in mines, mining
operations and mining securities. It goes into every
town and mining camp in New Mexico and
Arizona and is sold on the trains 450
miles west of Albuquerque.

SECOND STREET AND SILVER AVE.

Holden, S. S., carpenter, A. & P. shops.
Holmes, J. M., clerk, cashier's office, A. & P. railroad.
Home Fire Insurance Co., of New York, Charles Etheridge, agent.
Hondard, J. B., residence west end.
Hoover, A. F., south Fourth st., near Lead ave.
Horner, John, conductor, A , T. & S. F. railroad.
Hope, Jas. G., proprietor Armijo hotel.
Hope, Loyd H., boards at Armijo hotel.
Hope, Frank G., boards at Armijo hotel.
Hope, James D , boards at Armijo hotel.
Hopkins, R. W., book-keeper, Putney & Trask.
Hopkins, John, clerk, Phelps & Bennett.
Houston, C. J., waiter, Railroad ave.
Howe, Harry J., foreman Review.
Howe, E. S., chief of police.
Howe, C. H., jeweler, Railroad ave., bet. First and Second sts.
Howe, M. E., jeweler, Railroad ave., bet. First and Second sts.
Howard, Frank, residence west end.
Hubbs, C. L., manager Gran Quivera smelter, one mile south of city.
Hubbs, G. H., foreman, Gran Quivera smelter, one mile south of city.
Huettenmueller, John, clerk, Jaffa Bros., general merchandise.
Hughart, W. J., blacksmith, Albuquerque Foundry and Machine Co.
Hughes, Miles, blacksmith, A. & P. shops.
Hughes, Thomas, postmaster.
Huning, F., general merchandise, west end.
Huning, C., general merchandise, west end.
Hunt, E., manager Maden hotel.
Hurst, F. O., manager Western Union Telegraph Co.
Hurst, A. D., operator, A., T. & S. F. railroad office.
Hutchinson, R. N., book-keeper Review.
Hyman & Co., general merchandise, First st., bet. Railroad and Gold aves.
Hynes, Ed., boiler maker, A. & P. shops.

I

Ilfeld, Louie, Ilfeld & Co , general merchandise, First st., between Silver and Lead aves.
Ilfeld, Noah, Ilfeld & Co., general merchandise, First st., between Silver and Lead aves.
Iris, B. H., carpenter, A. & P. shops.
Isherwood, Thomas, foreman Albuquerque Foundry and Machine Co.
Irving, Will. residence west end.
Irony, Thomas, residence Highland addition.

J

Jacoby, D., machinist, A. & P. round house.
Jacoby, J. A., machinist, A. & P. round house.
Jachrin, J. J., residence west end.
Jewett, Charles, conductor A. & P. railroad, boards at Armijo hotel.

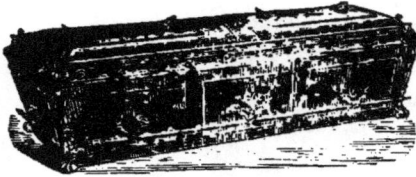

E. C. MONFORT

Undertaker

Metallic and Wood Cloth-Covered

⊰CASES ‡ AND ‡ CASKETS⊱

Garments, Coffins and Trimmings.

Attention Given to Embalming and Preserving Bodies.

Orders received for Monuments and Head Stones.

☞ A full line of SHOW CASES on Hand ☜

First Street, 3 Doors from Silver Ave.,   Albuquerque, N. M.

THE ALBUQUERQUE

DAILY DEMOCRAT

Neatest, Newsiest and Best Paper in the Territory

The Only Evening Paper in the Territory Publishing the Associated Press Dispatches. and

THE ⧫ ONLY ⧫ DEMOCRATIC ⧫ DAILY ⧫ IN ⧫ NEW ⧫ MEXICO

It is Democratic to the core, and is a fearless exponent of the principles of the Party. Its local and mining columns are excelled by no paper in the Territory.

Daily, $10 a Year.   **Weekly, $3 a Year.**

☞ The Democrat Job Office is more thoroughly equipped than any in the Southwest.

J. G. ALBRIGHT, Editor and Manager.

Jennings, G. W., foreman round house, A. & P. railroad.
Jesup, George, residence west end.
Jerme, W. H., carpenter, Lead ave., bet. Second and Third sts.
Johns, B. K., machinist, A. & P. round house.
Johnson, L., carpenter, Whitcomb & Medler.
Johnson, --, cook, A. & P. hospital.
Johnson, - -, foreman carpenters, A. & P.
Johnson, A., carpenter, A. & P. shops.
Johnson, George, car repairer, A. & P. shops.
Johnson, Ed., barber, south Second st.
Johnson, H. W., Bell & Co., Cyclone grocery.
Johnson, Cris., tinner, Vose & Co.
Johnson, J. F., harness and saddels, cor. Copper ave. and Second st.
Johnson, C., residence west end.
Johnson, W. B., residence west end.
Johnson, T. H., residence west end.
Johnson, Dr. W. H., physician and surgeon, over Frisco restaurant, R. R. ave.
Johnson, George, barber, St. Julien.
Journal Hotel, Silver ave., bet. First and Second sts.
Jones, C. C., machinist, A & P. round house.
Jones, W. D., boards at Armijo hotel.
Jones, John, harness and saddle maker, Second st., between Railroad and Copper aves.
Jones, Charles, painter, Silver ave., bet. Second and Third sts.
Jones, L. W., night watchman, A. & P. yards.
Jones, H. A., head clerk master carpenters, A. & P. shops.
Jones, C. P., Albuquerque Dairy, two miles north of town.
Jones, F. A., cook, Frisco restaurant.
Jobas, C. R., residence west end.
Judson, J., pipe-fitter, A. & P. shops.
Juillard, H. G., boot and shoe maker, First st. and Gold ave.

K

Katz, Albert, saloon, First st., bet. Copper and Railroad aves.
Kalihan, Mike, messenger Wells, Fargo & Co's. Express.
Kennedy, John W., Railroad Palace saloon, First st.
Kennedy, T. H., livery and sale stable, First st., bet Railrood and Copper aves.
Kenedy, C. W., Baca addition, near A. & P. general offices.
Kent, F. H., real estate, south Third st., bet. Railroad and Gold aves.
Keenan, James, carpenter, west end.
Kempenich, D., clerk, Max Schulster, west end.
Keane, Frank, car repairer, A. & P. shops.
Keleher, Thomas, hides, pelts and wool, Railroad ave. between Fourth and Fifth sts.
Kimball, Dr., physician and surgeon, cor. Second st. and Railroad ave.
Kimball, Charles, residence west end.
Kimball, C H., book-keeper, Stover, Crary & Co.
King, Arthur, cook, Journal hotel.

King, A., bartender, west end
Kirkland, Dr., room 3, McKinney building.
Kirck, Math, bartender Star saloon, west end.
Kirch, M., residence west end.
Killen, James, fireman, A. & P. railroad.
Kissling, Gus, cook, Oriental restaurant, south Second st.
Kistler, Rev. W. R., pastor Methodist church, house on Silver ave., bet. Fourth and Fifth sts.
Kitchen, Thomas, residence west end.
Kingman, Lewis, chief engineer, A. & P. railroad.
Kilpatrick, J. R., cashier Stover, Crary & Co.
Kilgore, Thomas P., undertaker, three doors from Silver ave. on First st.
Kiteler, T. H., residence west end.
Kinney, Charles, clerk, Marble hall.
Kline, T. S., Pegram & Kline, plumbers, cor. Silver ave. and Second st.
Kleinworth, Wm., beef contractor, Frank Armijo addition.
Kline, D. W., auctioneer, Favor & Co., Railroad ave., bet. First and Second sts.
Knisely, J., proprietor Los Angeles house, cor. Third st. and Silver ave.
Knox, Wm., boilermaker, A. & P. shops.
Knapp, A., laborer, A. & P. shops.
Knapp, G. R., yard master, A. & P. railroad.
Knight, O., blacksmith, A. & P. shops.
Kopenhoeffer, B. F., carpenter, A. & P. shops.
Koppe, A., blacksmith, Copper ave., bet. First and Second sts.
Konantz, J. A., salesman, Bell & Co., groceries.
Komberg, Louis, general merchandise, west end.
Kraft, Charles, E., clerk, Third st., bet. Gold and Silver aves.
Kreiger. John, carpenter, Copper ave. and Fourth st.
Kuhn, T. L., blacksmith, A. & P. shops.

L

Lafane, E., waiter, Frisco restaurant.
Lee, Miss Frankie, boards at Alameda house.
Lake, W. H., cor. south Fourth st. and Silver ave.
Lambert, J., barber, Railroad ave., bet. Second and Third sts.
Lamphier, E. A., H. Maden & Co., Gold ave.
Lamparter, C., wagon maker, Copper ave.
Langerman, S., clerk, Hyman & Co.
Lane, J. W., night clerk, Journal hotel.
Lang, James A., book-keeper, J. A. Lee & Co.
Larkin, W. D., Railroad ave., between First and Second sts.
Larson, John, machinist, A. & P. shops.
Lardner, A., baker, First st., bet. Railroad and Copper aves.
Larson, A., mill hand, A. & P.
Latta, Judge, capatalist, Second st., near A. & P. office.
Lawson, J. H., cashier, A., T. & S. F. railroad office.
Leas, George, clerk, J. E. Saint & Co.
Lee, H. M., compositor, Review.

Lee, John A., wholesale and retail lumber, glass, etc., corner Silver avenue and First st.

Lee, Alexander, passenger engineer, A. & P.

Leiser, Ed, bartender, Charles Zeiger.

Leitz, Joe, head-cook, Armijo hotel.

Lemon, A. G., brakeman, A. & P.

Leonhardt, Wm., patern-maker, A. & P.

Leonhardt, Carl, upholster, A. & P.

Leonard, W. C., Leonard & Young, general merchandise, First st., between Railroad and Gold aves.

Leonard, James, tinner, Vose & Co.

Leonard, John, compositor, Democrat.

Leroy, Mrs. A., dress maker, corner Copper ave. and Third st.

Leroy, Arthur, pedler, corner Copper ave. and Third st.

Lesser, D., proprietor Lesser Bros., Railroad ave., bet. Second and Third sts.

Lesser, L., proprietor Lesser Bros., Railroad ave., bet. Second and Third sts.

Levine, L., Levine & Randall, proprietors Oriental restaurant.

Lewis, H. C., Lewis & Ulman, proprietors Star clothing house, Railroad ave., between Second and Third sts.

Lewis, Miss Bell, dressmaker, corner Gold ave. and Fourth st.

Lewis, Miss Mary, dressmaker, corner Gold ave. and Fourth st.

Lewis, J. G., general merchandise, First st., bet. Railroad and Gold aves.

Lewis, C. W., general merchandise, First st., bet. Railroad and Gold aves.

Lewis, Chas., W., general merchandise, Main st., west end.

Liot, Louis, cook, Railroad ave., bet. First and Second sts.

Liverpool, London & Globe Fire Insurance Co., Charles Etheridge, agent.

Lightfoot, Dr. F., office Rio Grande hotel.

Linnenfelser, F. C., third clerk, A., T., & S. F. Railroad Co.

Longrisch, John, steam laundry, corner Second and Tijeras sts.

Lobata, L., residence west end.

Lobato, Pedro, residence west end.

Lobato, Antonio, residence west end.

Lobato, O., residence west end.

Lobato, Pitacio, residence west end.

Lobato, E., residence west end.

Locke, W., proprietor Oasis saloon, Railroad ave., bet. Second and Third sts.

Locke, E., laborer, A. & P.

Lowenthal, F., proprietor Frisco restaurant.

Loebner, Max, billiard palace, corner Third st. and Gold ave.

Long, Charles, residence west end.

London Assurance of London, Charles Etheridge, agent.

Lopez, José, 3d, residence west end.

Lopez, Pedro Clete, residence west end.

Lopez, José, 2d, residence west end.

Lopez, Federico, residence west end.

Lopez, Antonio, 1st., residence west end.

Lopez, H., residence west end.

Lopez, José D., residence west end.

MARIANO ARMIJO.   ELIAS ARMIJO.   JOHN BORRADAILE.

Armijo Brothers & Borradaile

REAL ESTATE

—— AND ——

Bernalillo County Abstract Office

→ MINES, INSURANCE AND MONEY BROKERS →

CONVEYANCERS AND NOTARIES.

Deeds Executed in either the English or Spanish Language

Take full Charge of Properties, Pay Taxes and Collect Rents.

MUNROE BUILDING, THIRD STREET

ALBUQUERQUE, N. M.

Armijo Brothers & Borradaile take full charge of Properties, pay and collect Rents.

Lopez, Pedro, residence west end.

Lopez, Manuel, residence west end.

Lopez, C., laborer, A. & P. shops.

Lopez, Asiano, residence west end.

Lovejoy, Frank, bartender, First st., near A. & P. shops.

Love, Wm., hostler, City livery stable, corner Fourth st. and Copper ave.

Lowson, Jack, Brown & Lowson, Santa Fe lunch counter, at depot.

Lucas, Carabajal, residence west end.

Ludnick, J. L., painter, A. & P.

Ludnick, H. M., painter, A. & P.

Luffer, O. G., brakeman, A. & P.

Lureno, Lucas, residence west end.

Lureno, Jesus, residence west end.

Lureno, José, residence west end.

Lureno, Antonio, residence west end.

Lureno, Y., residence west end.

Lusero, Trinidad, residence west end.

Luth, G. E., butcher, Gold ave., bet. Second and Third sts.

Lyman, H., brakeman, A. & P.

Lytle, Wm., tinner, Vose & Co.

Lyon, Dr. W. B., physician and surgeon, Third st. and Copper ave.

Lyons, J. B., residence Fruit ave.

Lyons, W. C., printer at Journal job office.

M

Mack, M. J., civil engineer, Gold ave, opp. Central bank.

Mack, Miss Lousia, chambermaid, Journal hotel.

Macbeth, Wm., Bradley & Macbeth, dentists, First st., between Railroad and Gold aves.

Madden, Wm., car repairer, A. & P.

Maden, H., H. Maden & Co., wholesale and retail crockery, glassware, etc., Gold ave., between First and Second sts.

Maden, E., H. Maden & Co., two doors from post office.

Magley, George J , mining editor Democrat.

Magill, George, shoe maker, Railroad ave., between First and Second sts.

Magis, J., blacksmith, A. & P.

Mandell, S., clerk, Stein, Mandell & Co.

Mandell, F., Stein, Mandell & Co., wholesale hardware, First st., between Railroad and Gold aves.

Maxwell, Joe, fireman, Albuquerque Gas Co.

Mandell, M., clerk, Ilfeld & Co., general merchandise.

Matta, F. S., editor La Revista.

Mathews, Clarance S., compositor Democrat.

Manning, E. W., laborer, A., T. & S. F. railroad.

Martine, Mariano, proprietor Star saloon, west end.

Martin, Mariano, residence west end.

Martin, Sallador, residence west end.

Martin, Roman, residence west end.

Martin, Manuel, residence west end.
Martin, Jesus, residence west end.
Martin, José, 1st, residence west end.
Martin, Juan, residence west end.
Martin, Bisente, residence west end.
Martin, Frank, freight engineer, A. & P.
Martin, F. E., car repairer, A. & P.
Martin, Antonio, residence west end.
Martin, Trinidad, residence west end.
Martin, Samuel, carpenter, E. Nichols, corner First st. and Silver ave.
Martin, E. S., compositor Review.
Martin, W. J., carpenter, A. & P. shops.
Martin, W. J., carpenter, A. & P. shops.
Martin, C. A., clerk, Wells, Fargo & Co.
Marrinan, Lawrence, proprietor Journal hotel, Silver ave., between First and Second sts.
Marshall, J. C., foreman pattern makers, A. & P.
Marcott, M. C., clerk, W. E. Talbott, corner Second st. and Railroad ave.
Marks, Ed, core-maker, Albuquerque Foundry & Machine Co.
Masters, Q. A., Masters & Walker, saloon, First st.
Matta, Lauro, jeweler, Santago st., west end.
Maybee, L., Maybee & Schaffer, jewelers, Second st., between Railroad and Gold aves.
May, Harry, residence west end.
McAnary, James, mason, west end.
McAdams, Wm., draftsman, A. & P. offices.
McClelan, W. N., McClelan & Rausch, meat market, Railroad ave., between First and Second sts.
McCottell, Joe, stage carpenter, opera house.
McComas, Judge C. C., Tijeras st. near Fifth.
McCauley, J. H., brakeman, A. & P. railroad.
McCarty, Joseph, cook, Journal hotel.
McClaskey, G. H., saddler, north Second st
McClure, John S., foreman John A. Lee & Co.
McCreight, W. T., foreman Democrat.
McCarty, Pat, waiter, Armijo hotel.
McDonald, J. F., McDonald Bros., blacksmiths, north Second st.
McDonald, M. A., McDonald Bros., blacksmiths, north Second st.
McDonald, J. S., corner Gold ave. and south Fifth st.
McElaney, James, boilermaker, A. & P.
McFarren, J., boot and shoe maker, First st., between Railroad and Gold aves.
McGinnis, Wm., residence west end.
McGrath, Miss Lizzie, Vine cottage, Copper ave.
McGuire, D. C., brick contractor, Highland addition.
McGuire, Wm., contractor and builder.
McIntosh, D. W., contractor and builder, boards at Rio Grande hotel.
McKenzie, Andy D., saloon, Second st., between Railroad and Copper aves.
McKenna, Ed, moulder, Albuquerque Foundry and Machine Co.

McLane, Charles, blacksmith, A. & P.

McLean, M. F., boards at Armijo hotel.

McLean, John, moulder, Albuquerque Foundry and Machine Co.

McMindes, Miss Lizzie, dressmaker, Second st. and Lead ave.

McKee, M. A., Peterson & McKee, Mountaineer billiard parlor.

McMartin, Mrs., proprietress Delmonico restaurant, west end.

McNamara, John, proprietor saloon, First st., near A. & P. shops.

McPhail, James, foreman boilermakers, A. & P.

McPherson, Pete, driver, Scott & Borchert.

McPherron, Prof., teacher, Highland addition.

Medler, E., Whitcomb & Medler, contractors and builders, cor. First st. and Gold ave.

Medler, Mrs. E., millinery and fancy goods, Second st., between Gold and Silver aves.

Menaul, Rev. J. A., pastor Presbyterian church, house Gold ave., between Fifth and Sixth sts.

Messinger, Morris, residence Armijo addition.

Metzger, J., proprietor Gold Avenue meat market.

Myers, M. F., A. & P. bakery and groceries, near A. & P. shops.

Myers, R. B., residence Gold ave., bet. First and Second sts.

Mills, Wm., street car driver.

Mills, G. D., brakeman, A. & P.

Miles, Frank, clerk, Jewett house.

Miller, W. H., painter, Silver ave., between Second and Third sts.

Miller, Isaac, carpenter, Whitcomb & Medler.

Miller, Jacob, blacksmith, A. & P.

Miller, M. G., saloon, First st.

Miller, D. R., roofer, Third st., between Railroad and Gold aves.

Miller, I. A., boards at Journal hotel.

Miller, George, residence west end.

Mitchell, W. A., Scott & Borchert, furniture.

Mitchell, George, tinner, Vose & Co.

Mitchell, —, dishwasher, Girard house.

Mitclal, G., waiter, Railroad ave.

Mitmes. , blacksmith, A. & P. shops.

Montoya, Nesto, residence west end.

Montoya, E., residence west end.

Montoya, Hestor, residence west end.

Montoya, Manuel, laborer, A. & P. yards.

Monfort, H. A., undertaker, First st., between Silver and Lead aves.

Montrose, Miss Nellie, boards 555, Copper eve.

Montaldo, Charles, proprietor White House billiard parlor, Railroad ave., near Third st.

. Monroe, Mrs. Ida, millinery, Monroe building, Third st.

Monroe, George, proprietor saloon, Railroad ave., bet. Second and Third sts.

Moore, Joe, meat market, Gold ave.

Moore, Scott, capitalist and stockman, office Armijo Bros. & Borradaile.

Moe, Martin, porter, D L Sammis.

Morehead, Charles, chief clerk engineer's department, A. & P.
Morris, B., clerk, Jaffa Bros, general merchandise.
Morris, Miss Lillie, boards at Copper ave.
Morris, Miss Maggie, 555, Copper ave.
Morris, George, baker, west end.
Morrison, J. A., proprietor I X L laundry, corner First st, and Lead ave.
Morrison, J. A., undertaker, Torrey, Anderson & Sloan.
Morelli, D,, tailor, south Second st.
Morley, Miss Rye, chambermaid, Rio Grande hotel.
Morgan, Wm., carpenter, A. & P. shops.
Molt, R. E., machinist, A. & P.
Moshage, Wm., teamster, rooms Lead ave. and First st.
Moshier, George, carpenter, E. Nichols.
Moshgare, Wm , teamster, corner Lead ave, and First st.
Moses, B., cigars and tobacco, Railroad ave., bet. First and Second sts.
Mutual Life Insurance Co. of New York, Charles Etheridge, agent.
Muller, Jacob, saloon and lodging house, Railroad ave., between First and Second sts.
Munis, José, residence west end.
Murphy, James, residence west end.
Muzio, A., Prof. of languages, Highland addition.
Mulligan, R., helper, Albuquerque Gas Co.
Mustard, James, bartender, Jewett house.
Mullin, W. D., residence west end.
Murphy, M. G., lodging house, First st.
Muntz, Jasper, car repairer, A. & P.
Muehl, Dr. E., physician and surgeon, west end.
Mulligan, S. H., traveling agent, W. E. Talbott.
Moya, David, residence west end.
Moya, Jacob, residence west end.
Myers, Fred, fireman, A., T. & S. F. railroad.
Myers, Paddy, residence west end.

N

Nichols, J. W., route agent, Wells, Fargo & Co.
Nichols, T. E., Whitson & Nicols, music store, Second st.
Nicols, E., carpenter and builder, corner Silver ave. and First st.
Nigler, M., waiter, Rio Grande hotel.
Nemier, Frank, carpenter, Frank Armijo addition.
Nettleton, M. C., watchmaker, J. K. Basye
Nehr, George, saloon, west end.
Neill, John, machinist A. & P. shops.
Nelson, Joe, third cook, Rio Grande hotel.
Neustadt, S., Neustadt Bros., general mercdandise, corner Gold avenue and First st.
Neustadt, L., Neustadt Bros., general merchandise, corner Gold avenue and First st.
Neril, Jack, plumber, Pegram & Kline.

Neulin, Allen, messenger, Wells, Fargo & Co.
Neis, Tony, superintendent Rocky Mountain Detective Agency.
Neis, Albert, assistant superintendent Rocky Mountain Detective Agency.
Neylon, John, blacksmith, A. & P.
Nelan, Thomas, pipe-fitter, A. & P.
Nixon, W. C., agent A., T. & S. F. railroad.
Norris, Frank, saloon keeper, boards at Armijo hotel.
Norris, Wm., machinist, A. & P.
Northup, C. O., saloon, corner First st. and Copper ave.
Norman, C. R., plumber, Pegram & Kline.
Noble, W. W., butcher, Ellingwood & Adams.
Nolan, Harry, bartender, W. E. Talbott.
Nuthall, W. machinist, A. & P.

O

Oakeson, D. A., brakeman, A. & P.
Obanonn, Lewis, proprietor Cabinet saloon, west end.
Ogle, H. W., residence west end.
Ostergren G. A., photographer.
Ott, Charles D., bartender, Terrill & Parker.
Otero, M. S., president First National bank.
Otis, Antonio, residence west end.
Orink, Leonard, residence west end.
Owen, Charles, route agent, A. & P.
Owen, Arnet R., district attorney, room 5, Cromwell block, residence corner
Fifth and Marquette sts.
Ostrom, A. H., carpenter, boards at Lewis building.
Otero, Francisco Armijo, lawyer, west end.

P

Padwick, W. W., patternmaker, A. & P. shops.
Parfette, Joe, tailor, Second st., bet. Gold and Silver aves.
Parker, A. L., engineer, A. & P.
Parkinson, Al, freight engineer, A. & P.
Parkinson, John, machinist, A. & P.
Parker, S., Maden hotel saloon.
Passmore, Charles, laborer, A., T. & S. F. railroad.
Patterson, L. L., blacksmith, north Second st.
Patten, W. H., superintendent A. & P. Coal Co.
Patten, Miss S., assistant matron Albuquerque Indian school.
Patten, Miss M. H., matron Albuquerque Indian school.
Paulson, Richard, draftsman, A. & P.
Pearce, F. L., wholesale lumber dealer, Highland addition.
Pechner Alex, Goldstein & Pechner, proprietors Boston clothing house, Railroad
ave., bet. Second and Third sts.
Pegram, W. D., Pegram & Kline, plumbers.
Pennsylvania Fire Insurance Co. of Philadelphia, Charles Etheridge, agent.
Perea, Meliton, residence west end.

Perea, Miguel, residence west end.

Perea, Jesus, residence west end.

Perea, José, residence west end.

Perea, Filipe, residence west end.

Perea, Francisco, residence west end.

Perea, Ygnacia, residence west end.

Plozone, Carlos, residence west end.

Peterson, Louis, Peterson & McKee, proprietors Mountaineer billiard hall.

Peterson, A., machinist, A. & P.

Petre, Oswald, soda manufacturer, Frank Armijo addition.

Phelps, A. H., hostler, City livery stable.

Phellips, Dr., corner Second st. and Lead ave.

Phillips, Z. P., car accountant, A. & P. railroad.

Phelps, R. S., Phelps & Bennett, clothing, Railroad ave., between Second and Third sts.

Phelan, James, janitor A. & P. railroad.

Phelan, Tom F., residence west end.

Phelan, John C., Pinger & Phelan, druggists, cor. Railroad ave. and Second st.

Phœnix Fire Insurance Company, of London, Charles Etheridge, agent.

Pierce, C F., clerk probate court, west end.

Pillsbury, G. S., Pillsbury Bros., druggists, corner Third st. and Railroad ave.

Pillsbury, O S., corner Third st. and Railroad ave.

Pickett, H L., attorney at law.

Pinkham, George B, proprietor St. Julien saloon, corner Railroad ave. and Second st.

Pischenot, Mrs., grocery, Railroad ave., between Second and Third sts.

Pratt, Harry S., manager of the Albuquerque, Las Vegas and Santa Fe Business Directory.

Pratt, F. G., Dobson & Pratt, groceries, Highland addition.

Pratt, James, corner Second and Tijeras sts.

Prager, William S., residence west end.

Priest, Ed, proprietor Elk saloon, Railroad ave., between First and Second sts.

Pringle, C A., carpenter E. Nichols.

Prissner, F. B., carpenter, Highland addition.

Prizell, John, carpenter A. & P.

Price, John K., president Albuquerque Foundry and Machine Company, boards Armijo hotel.

Price, R R., railroad contractor, boards Armijo hotel.

Price, G W., compositor Review.

Prickett, George, car repairer A. & P.

Pringle, James, carpenter E. Nichols.

Post, F. D., general merchandise, end of Rio Grande bridge.

Pohl, George, wiper A. & P. shops.

Ponsell, F A., residence west end.

Potter, Miss Mary, dressmaker.

Porter, Oliver, street car driver.

Porner, Joseph, bakery, west end.

Poundstone, J. D, assistant dispatcher A. & P.

Putney, L. B., Putney & Trask, wholesale groceries, corner First st. and Railroad ave.

Q

Quinn, T. G., assistant dispatcher A. & P.

Quinn, Barney, bartender Oasis saloon.

Quinn, F., cook Armijo hotel.

Queer, Peter, carpenter, Highland addition.

Quetil, Charles, civil engineer, Third st., between Railroad and Gold aves.

R .

Raff, Norman C., assistant cashier Central bank.

Raynolds, J. C., president Central bank.

Ramsey, A. J., boards Journal hotel.

Randell, J. W., teamster, house on Second st., between Lead and Silver aves.

Randell, J. B., architect and superintendent, postoffice box 141.

Randall, John, Levines & Randall, Oriental restaurant.

Rankin, E. R., clerk at Dr. Easterday's.

Ratcliff, M. J., second hand store, corner Second st. and Gold ave.

Rausch, Fred, McClelan & Rausch, meat market, Railroad ave., between First and Second streets.

Raymond, J. L., blacksmith A. & P.

Reed, E. A., books, stationery and news depot, Gold ave., between First and Second sts.

Reed, George, brakeman A. & P.

Reed, Fred, waiter Rio Grande hotel.

Reese, R. M., residence west end.

Reese, Frank, billiard parlor, corner Third st. and Gold ave.

Reese, Samuel, street car driver.

Refugio, L., porter Journal hotel.

Reed, A. K., waiter Frisco restaurant, Railroad ave.

Reimer, D., carpenter A. & P. yards.

Renick, Robert, driver Wells, Fargo & Co.

Rhinehart, J. T. Van Slyck & Rhinehart, proprietors Kansas Store, general merchandise.

Ribble, Henry H., Silver ave., between south Third and Fourth streets.

Ridley, Malh, boilermaker A. & P. shops.

Richardson, J. W., carpenter A. & P. shops.

Richmond, Harry, marshal west end.

Rickards, D., bartender, boards Los Angeles house.

Riley, Ed, bartender Marble hall.

Riley, John, Highland addition.

Riley, John, mason, rooms Dawson lodging house.

Riley, Frank, Bean & Riley, spring bed manufactory, Gold ave., between Fourth and Fifth sts.

Roberts, J. O., day clerk, Armijo hotel.

Roberts, S. A., tinner, Vose & Co.

Roberts, S. C., foreman tinners, Vose & Co.

Robertson, H. C., clerk, Ballingall house.

Robinson, Charles, house corner Fourth st.. near Lead ave.
Rodey, Bernard, real estate and notary public, room 5, Cromwell block.
Rodriges, Roman, residence west end.
Rood, C. L., foreman material yards, A. & P.
Rogers, J. S., brakeman, A. & P.
Romero, Andres, residence west end.
Romero, José, residence west end.
Romero, Perfecto, residence west end.
Romero, Jesus, residence west end.
Romero, Felis, residence west end.
Romero, J., laborer, A. & P.
Romero, Garcia, clerk, R. J. Sanches, west end.
Romero, T., T. Romero & Son, general merchandise, Gold ave., between First and Second sts.
Romero, S., T. Romero & Son, general merchandise, Gold ave., between First and Second sts.
Ronan, Charles, boards at Armijo hotel.
Ront, Wm., grocery and saloon, Railroad ave., near west end.
Ross, N., carpenter, A. & P. shops.
Ross, E. J., editor Democrat.
Rosehall, Thomas, carpenter, A. & P.
Rosenthal, Louie, city editor Democrat.
Rosenkakranz, Charles, book-keeper, Staab & Co.
Rowley, George, car inspector, A. & P.
Russ, Dr. physician and surgeon, Railroad ave., near west end.
Ruis, Manuel, residence west end.
Ruis, Francisco, residence west end.
Ruis, Mariano, residence west end.
Ruple, Capt. S., Third st. and Gold ave.
Ruppe, Bernhard, drugs and toilet articles, west end.
Russell, C., laborer, A. & P.
Russell, R. W., photographer, Gold ave., between First and Second sts.
Russ, Mason, blacksmith, A. & P. shops.
Rutherfue, A., carpenter, Highland addition.

S

Salles, George, waiter, Journal hotel.
Sandoval, P. M., clerk, Lesser Bros.
Sass, Pete, carpenter, Whitcomb & Medler.
Sanders, C. W., chief engineer's office, A. & P.
Sanders, W. C., chief clerk chief engineer's office, A. & P.
Saunders, James T., attorney at law, room 5, Cromwell block.
Saunders, W. F., editor Review.
Sammis, D. L., commission and fowarding merchant, cor. First st. and Gold ave.
Sanches, Nicholas, residence west end.
Sanches, Ed, painter, A. & P.
Sanches, N. J., general merchandise, west end.
Sawyer, E. A., clerk, Lesser Bros., general merchandise.

ALBUQUERQUE DIRECTORY. 73

Sanches, C. N., clerk, T. Romero & Son, general merchandise.

Sanches, D., residence west end.

Sandobal, Pedro, residence west end.

Sandobal, Francisco, residence west end.

Santillanes, Juan, residence west end.

Sawyer, Dr. Z. B., physician and surgeon, Tijeras st., between Fourth and Fifth sts.

Scanderett, H. A., clerk freight office, A & P.

Schmidt, F., clerk, F. Huning, general merchandise, west end.

Scholenberger, L., laborer, A. & P. shops.

Scholenberger, J. D., carpenter, A. & P.

Schuster, Max, general merchandise, west end.

Schaffer, W. W., book-keeper, Vose & Co.

Schaffer, H., Maybee & Schaffer, jewelers, Second st., between Railroad and Gold aves.

Schmidt, F., clerk, Staab & Co., general merchandise.

Schlerth, George, Vose & Co., hardware, First st.

Schuler, W. N., clerk, Santa Fe lunch counter, at depot.

Schroder, Wm., street car driver.

Scott, Mrs. Mary, Scott & Borchert, wholesale furniture, First st.

Scott, Edward, jeweler, west end.

Scotty, Joe, mason, Copper ave., between Sixth and Seventh sts.

Scottish Union & National Fire Insurance Co., of Edinburgh and London, Chas. Etheridge, agent.

Scroder, C., laborer, A. & P. shops.

Scrader, Wm., street car driver, west end.

Scrader, Charles, baker, corner First st and Silver ave.

Sedgwick, T. S., land commissioner, A. & P. office.

Sedillo, Emitenio, residence west end.

Sedillo, Jnan, residence west end.

Segra, Charles, waiter, west end.

Seller, Charles C., corner Railroad ave. and Second st.

Sena, George, driver, Bell & Co.

Sena, Pedro, residence west end.

Serbantes, José, residence west end.

Seth, Smith, clerk, Staab & Co., general merchadise.

Sharick, I. J., manufacturing jeweler, diamonds, watches and silverware, Railroad ave., bet. Second and Third sts.

Sharick, P., clerk, I. J. Sharick, jeweler.

Shay, R., residence west end.

Shaw, James, residence west end.

Shaw, E., residence west end.

Sheffel, Wm., painter, A. & P. shops.

Shepperd, Rev. Wm. Y., pastor Methodist Church South, residence cor. Silver ave. and Fourth st.

Sheetz, F., head clerk, A., T. & S. F. railroad office.

Sheeham, J. P., baggage master, A., T. & S. F. railroad.

Shelman, A. A., Oasis saloon, Railroad ave., bet. Second and Third sts.

Sharp, John, clerk, F. Huning, general merchandise, west end.
Shackrow, Wm., patten maker, A. & P. shops.
Sharp, H., car repairer, A. & P.
Shinnick, T. J., secretary Albuquerque Street Railroad Co., residence west end.
Shoaf, Simon, helper, A. & P. shops.
Sholtz, A. H., second clerk, A., T. & S. F. railroad office
Shultz, C. M., business manager Journal.
Sigwalt, J., waiter, restaurant, Railroad ave.
Sing, Wing, laundry, between Silver and Lead aves.
Singer, W. F., clerk, B. Moses, Railroad ave., bet. First and Second sts.
Simon, J. M., saloon, west end.
Simons, Jake, Second st. and Lead ave.
Simple, Adam, porter, A. & P. shops.
Simons, S., Simons & Walker, Franz Huning's addition, near A. & P. shops.
Simpson, Fred, machinist A. & P. shops.
Skinner, Miss Mary, waiter, Rio Grande hotel.
Slaughter, W J., proprietor barber shop, Armijo hotel.
Slaughter, Charles, barber, Armijo hotel.
Slanghter, J., clerk, E. J. Post & Co., Railroad ave.
Sleight, W. W., carpenter, Highland addition.
Sloan, A. C., Torrey, Anderson & Sloan, furniture.
Smith, John, plumber and gas fitter.
Smith, J. E., New Mexico Emporium, west end.
Smith, W. A., proprietor New Mexico Emporium, west end.
Smith, Edmond, clerk district court, west end.
Smith, W. A., grocery, west end.
Smith, F., clerk, B. Spitz, general merchandise, west end.
Smith, Guss, blacksmith, house on Copper ave., bet. First and Second sts.
Smith, James, cook, Armijo hotel.
Smith, Oscar, restaurant, north First st.
Smith, W. N., proprietor New Mexico Novelty works, Third st.
Smith, F. F., foreman E. Nichols, cor. Silver ave. and First st.
Smith, Jim, waiter, Jewett house.
Smith, F. W., general superintendent A. & P. railroad.
Smith, C. B., contractor, A., T. & S. F. railroad.
Smith, James R., miller, corner Ninth st. and Lead ave.
Smith, J. A., residence west end.
Smith, Wm., residence west end.
Smith, F., clerk, W. E. Talbott.
Smith, J. J., barber, Railroad ave., between Second and Third sts,
Smitz, Phillip, saloon, west end.
Small, Charles, waiter, Frisco restaurant.
Snyder, K. A., attorney at law, Third st., bet. Railroad and Gold aves.
Snow, H. C., painter, A. & P.
Snowden, F. H., collector Journal.
Soikes, D., waiter, Frisco restaurant.
Soto, Lisilio, residence west end.
Spencer, E. W., clerk, Pillsbury & Co., corner Railroad ave. and Third st.

Spellacy, John, boilermaker, A. & P.

Spear, Miss Blanche, boards at 555, Copper ave.

Springfield Fire & Marine Insurance Co. of Mass., Charles Etheridge, agent.

Spooner, Mrs. C. L., millinery and dressmaker, Third st., bet. Railroad and Copper aves.

Spitz, B., general merchandise, west end

Spitz, Edward, Staab & Co., general merchandise, Central bank building.

Squaies, W. H., carpenter, A. & P.

Staab, A., Staab & Co., general merchandise, Central bank building.

Staab, Z., Staab & Co., general merchandise, Central bank building.

Standard Fire Office of London, Charles Etheridge, agent.

Stamm, George, Second st., bet. Fourth and Fifth sts.

Starkweather, Burt, clerk, New York clothing store, Railroad avenue, between First and Second sts.

St. Clair, Miss Allie, boards at 87 Copper ave.

Stevens, E. A., milkman, Highland addition.

Stein, Max, groceries, Gold ave., bet. First and Second sts.

Stevenson, H. S., carpenter, Whitcomb & Medler, cor. Gold ave. and First st.

Stewart, George, brakeman, A. & P. railroad.

Stearns, DeWitte, attorney at law, Lewis' building, First st.

Stinson, J. W., clerk, Leonard & Young, general merchandise.

Stein, C. A., Stein, Mandell & Co., hardware, First st., between Railroad and Gold aves.

Stewart, Charles, porter, Ballingall house.

Stever, Charles, manager New Mexico Novelty Works.

Stevenson, J P., tailor, Railroad ave., bet. First and Second sts.

Steavenson, N. E., residence west end.

Strong, C. H., Strong Bros., second hand store, Copper ave., between Second and Third sts.

Strong, O. W., Strong Bros., second hand store.

Strass, H., book-keeper, Speigelberg Bros.

Strasburg, Ed, painter, Silver ave., between Second and Third sts.

Stone, George, porter, Stover, Crary & Co.

Stoepel, II. E., clerk, A. & P. general offices.

Stover, E. S., Stover, Crary & Co., wholesale groceries.

Stoner, A. M., carpenter, A. & P shops.

Stone, W. S., Whiteman & Stone, attorneys at law, cor. Second st. and Gold ave.

Sullivan, John II., lawyer, office Monroe building, Third st.

Sullivan, Hugh, First st., near A. & P. offices.

Sullivan, J. H., Jr., boards at Rio Grande hotel.

Surrey, C., waiter, Armijo hotel.

Sumerlin, J F., artist, Albright's parlor, Gold ave.

Summers, James A., books and stationery, cor. Second st. and Gold ave.

Sullivan, D. J., justice of the peace, office cor. Railroad ave. and Second st., up stairs.

Sullivan, M. L., blacksmith, A. & P. shops.

Surran, R., barber, Railroad ave., between Second and Third sts.

Suttington, Green, porter, Rio Grande house.

Swanson, John, carpenter, A. & P.

Swayzee, Miss J. H., cashier H. Maden & Co

Swygart, J. W., Carpenter & Swygart, painters, Second st., bet. Railroad and Copper aves.

T

Taber, Charles G., book-keeper, Central bank.

Terral, L. L., clerk chief engineer's office, A. & P.

Telerman, Wm., painter, A. & P. shops.

Tedrone, F. W., residence west end.

Tessier, L. A., barber, Railroad ave., bet. First and Second sts.

Taylor, D., foreman Journal job office.

Taylor, G. L., Whitcomb & Medler, cor. First st. and Gold ave.

Taylor, Thomas, residence west end.

Tams, H., city circulator, Review.

Talbott, W. E., wholesale liquor dealer, cor. Railroad ave. and Second st.

Talbot, Fred, R., Tucker, Taddis & Co., contractors and builders, and brick yard.

Tarbox, J. B., merchant tailor, Second st., bet. Railroad and Gold aves.

Tabolla, F., residence west end.

Taddis, P. C., Tucker, Taddis & Co., brick yards.

Tibbals, Mrs. L. B., teacher Albuquerque Indian school.

Thompson, W. W., cook, Retreat restaurant, west end.

Thompson, Wm., Thompson, Stamm & Co, groceries, Gold ave.

Thomas, B. H., carpenter, A. & P. shops.

Thompson, T. B., carpenter, A. & P. shops.

Thompson, W. W., residence west end.

Thompson, Frank, clerk, J. E. Saint & Co.

Thomas, Dr. J. H., Silver ave , bet. Fourth and Fifth sts.

Thornton, W. T., attorney at law, cor. Gold ave. and Second st.

Thorton, P., Oasis saloon, Railroad ave.

Torrey, J. S., Torrey, Anderson & Sloan, furniture, First st., between Railroad and Gold aves.

Torlina, George, E., general merchandise, Gold ave. bet. First and Second sts.

Toporoff, R., clerk, Jaffa Bros.

Toribro, C., residence west end.

Tones, Francisco, residence west end.

Toor, R., assistant cook, Rio Grand hotel.

Tox, Thomas, painter, A. & P. shops.

Trask, A. C., clerk Putney & Trask.

Trask, T. J., Putney & Trask, wholesale groceries, cor. Railroad ave. and First st.

Travelers Accident Insurance Co. of Hartford, Conn., Chas. Etheridge, agent.

Trauer, Sam, clerk, T. Romero & Son,

Trauer, Morris, Hyman & Co.

Trimble, W. S., proprietor livery stable, Second st., between Railroad and Copper aves.

Trimble, L. S., law office, west end.

Trimble, Charles, at W. S. Trimble & Co.

Torlicht, Gus, clerk, Stein, Mandell & Co.
Trumbull, W., Vose & Co., hardware, First st.
Trott, F. B., book-keeper, Jesse M. Wheelock.
Trujillo, José, porter, Putney & Trask.
Turner, E. L., compositor, Review
Tucker, J. H., Tucker, Taddis & Co., brick yards.
Tway, John, conductor, A, & P. railroad.
Tyler, James F., carpenter, A. & P. shops.

U

Uncupher, James, yard master, A.& P.
Upquhart, J. E., carpenter, A. & P.
Upington, Walter, J. K. Basye, Railroad ave., bet. Second and Third st.
Ulman, S. E., Lewis & Ulman, proprietors Star clothing house, Railroad ave., between Second and Third sts.
Uhlfelder, Julius, manager Rosenwold Bros,, cor, Railroad ave, and Third st.

V

Van Osdil, T. W., carpenter A. & P. shops.
Van Clere, D. D., passenger engineer A. & P.
Van Slyck, N., Van Slyck & Rhinehart, general merchandise, Gold ave., bet. First and Second streets.
Valencia, S., residence west end.
Van, William, residence west end.
Varley, John, residence west end.
Valencia, Sibeno, residence west end.
Varache, Eugene, St. Julien restaurant, Railroad ave., bet. Second and Third.
Vernon, Miss Trixie, star, opera house.
Verbeek, Miss S., seamstress Albuquerque Indian school.
Vegrard, M. E., tinner Stein, Mandell & Co.
Vose, R. C., Vose & Co., hardware, First st., between Gold and Silver aves.
Volz, F. W., carpenter A. & P. shops.
Viser, Ed, clerk postoffice.
Viser, Henry, clerk postoffice.

W

Waterman, T. H., Scott & Borchert, furniture.
Wade, P., rooms Munroe building.
Wade, Miss B., housekeeper Mrs. Aubright.
Wade, Thos., Boyd & Wade, opera house.
Watson, John, blacksmith A. & P. shops.
Walker, J R., operator Western Union Telegraph Company.
Walker, C., Masters & Walker, saloon, Railroad ave., near First st.
Walther, Charles, guns and revolvers, Second st., between Gold and Silver aves.
Walker, L., Simons & Walker, tannery, near A. & P. shops.
Walker, W. A., clerk Marble Hall.
Walker, A., bookkeeper J. E. Saint & Co.

Walker, W. M., residence west end.

Walton, W. Y., Aubright & Walton, druggists, Railroad ave., between Second and Third sts.

Walton, Harry, clerk Aubright & Walton.

Waldroris, W., cook Frisco restaurant.

Wainey, Charles, bartender Ballingall house.

Warde, L. L., route agent Wells, Fargo & Company.

Watson, Edward, day clerk Journal hotel.

Weaver, Charles, blacksmith, Copper ave., between Second and Third sts.

Weaver, H. E., brakeman A. & P.

Weishoff, Thomas, machinist A. & P.

Webb, C., storekeeper A. & P.

Webster, Arthur, compositor Democrat.

Weed, H. W., bartender, Railroad ave., between Second and Third sts.

Welson, G. W., residence west end.

Wells, A. G., head clerk general superintendent A. & P.

Weller, W. H., machinist A. & P.

Wells, Mrs. Mary, widow, south Third st., between Gold and Silver aves.

Wells, Miss Minerva, south Third st., between Gold and Silver aves.

Weiller, D., clerk Stein, Mandell & Co.

Wellman, A. L., carpenter Whitcomb & Medler.

Welker, C. R., compositor Review.

Weinman, J. A., clerk T. Romero & Son, general merchandise.

Weinman, S. A., residence west end.

Weisman, R., bartender, Railroad ave., between First and Second sts.

Werner, Thomas, residence west end.

Werner, Nicholas, probate clerk, west end.

Western Assurance Co., of Toronto, Charles Etheridge, agent.

Whalen, James, section hand, Highland addition.

Wheelock, J. M., architect and superintendent and real estate, corner Gold ave. and Second st.

Whitson, A. D., Whitson & Nichols, music store, Second st., between Railroad and Gold aves.

Whitney, Frank, Frank Armijo addition.

Whiteman, W. H., Whiteman & Stone, attorneys at law, corner Gold ave. and Second st.

Whitcomb, A. M., Whitcomb & Medler, contractors and builders, corner Gold ave. and First st.

Whitbeck, J. E., tinner Stein, Mandell & Co.

Wheelock, George F., manufacturer of galvanized iron cornice, office and shop Railroad ave. and Fourth st.

Wible, F. H., carpenter A. & P.

Wicks, R. M., operator A. T. & S. F. office.

Willis, E., fireman A. & P.

Willis, James, engineer switch engine A. & P.

Willey, H. S., proprietor Albuquerque flour mill, end of Lead ave.

Williams, Charles, car repairer A. & P.

Williams, James, brakeman A. & P.

Williams, R., stock ranch, Frank Armijo addition.

Williams, C. R., general freight and passenger agent A. & P.

Williams, George, residence west end.

Wilson, Francis, carpenter A. & P.

Wilson, W. K. P., cashier Central bank.

Wilson, Royal, head waiter Armijo hotel.

Willis, J. K., machinist A. & P.

Wilson, S. C., Vose & Co., hardware, First st.

Wilson, Jim, machinist Albuquerque Foundry and Machine Company.

Wilson, Jacob, moulder Albuquerque Foundry and Machine Company.

Wilson, A. B., secretary and treasurer Albuquerque Foundry and Machine Co.

Wilson, W.W., night clerk Rio Grande hotel.

Wilson, R. S., bartender, Railroad ave., between First and Second sts.

Wittick, Ben, Wittick & Russell, photographers, Gold ave., between First and Second st.

Winston, J., carpenter, First st., up stairs.

Winston, Mrs. A., dressmaker, First st., up stairs.

Winters, R. P., clerk cashier's office.

Wood, William, waiter Oriental restaurant.

Wood, E., Scott & Borchert.

Wood, A., E. J. Post & Co., hardware, First st.

Wood, Miss Mariette, teacher Albuquerque Indian school.

Woodruff, W. G., boards Armijo house.

Worth, J., freight engineer A. & P.

Wright, L., boards Armijo hotel.

Wright, William, machinist A. & P.

Wratten, George L., attorney at law and notary public, room 9 Cromwell block

Y

Yoast, Joe, Albuquerque Foundry and Machine Company.

Yanaway, C. L., carpenter A. & P. shops.

Yukey, Fred, boards Armijo hotel.

Young, E. W., Leonard & Young, general merchandise, First st., between Railroad and Gold aves.

Young, G. E., clerk Wells, Fargo & Company.

Z

Zeiger, Charles, wholesale liquor dealer, corner First st. and Railroad ave.

Zeiger, Gus, saloon west end.

Zeiger, Jacob, clerk Jaffa Bros., general merchandise, Railroad ave., between First and Second sts.

Zirhut, M. C., carriage maker, shops west end and Copper ave., between Second and Third sts.

LAS VEGAS.

Las Vegas, the county seat of San Miguel county, is located upon the banks of the river Gallinas, and contains, according to a recent census, something less than seven thousand souls.

The early history of the town is somewhat obscure, but before the territory became a part of the union what is now known as Upper Las Vegas was the trading point for miles away. For many years the town increased in growth but slowly, and indeed, not until the advent of the railroad did anyone imagine that it would ever reach the proportions and importance of a city. Nor was such a conclusion, in those days, unreasonable, for in the olden time New Mexico was practically, and in fact, unknown except in name. If now and then a free-lance Bohemian wandered into the far-off land, his descriptions of the land through which he traveled and the people that he saw, were not calculated to induce others to follow him.

Sensational writers had accepted New Mexico as the field of their fertile imaginations, and many a scene of rapine and murder had been pictured as occurring within her borders by their romantic pens. A state of semi-civilization was exaggerated into a condition of heathenish barbarism, and the usual occupation of most of the residents was described as closely resembling the calling of Dick Turpin or Rob Roy.

Not a kindley word of the country or habits of is people ever reached the outside world, and for long weary pears it was abandoned to the sloth of its primeval ways. The natives for the most part engaged in pastoral pursuits—living in quiet and peace as their ancestors lived; living as the patriarchs lived in the morning of the world. Children were born and old men passed away, but the rest remained unchanged. From some commanding knoll the herdsmen watched their flocks lazily browsing in the quiet valleys, or along the green banks of murmuring rivers; in the sequestered country home the mother washed and baked and sang a lullaby to her prattling child; in the curiously constructed and sleeply looking villages the merchant and postmaster sat in the doorway waiting for the incoming stage; at eventide the vesper bells broke the brooding silence, and in the white-washed chapels reverence knelt in prayer;

and across long stretches of mountain and desert, weary oxen drew enormous loads, coming from the States. These were the only signs of human habitation, and but for these the scene would have presented a country abandoned and forsaken.

This was the picture five years ago, but with the coming of the railroad all experienced a change and no where in the territory has the change been more rapid than in Las Vegas. In this city the one story adobe houses have given place to elegant and substantial structures of brick or stone. The work of building is rapidly going forward and the streets present an appearance well calculated to inspire the strongest confidence in its permanency and continued growth. You will find in the new city miles of side tracks, elegant and commodious offices of the management of the New Mexico division of the A. T. & S. F. R. R., mammoth wholesale and commission houses carrying stocks of millions of dollars. The hum of manufacturing industries will attract your attention. A line of street railway, water works, gas works and a telephone exchange will be found in operation.

The future of New Mexico, if written to-day, would be called an Aladdin's story; her possibilities are bewildering. A territory broader than Old and New England, whose mountains cover every shining metal, whose valleys are perfumed with every fruit and flower known to the temperate zone, is dawning upon the world. The elements that constitute financial greatness are hers, and when the approaching roads from Texas, Colorado and the Indian Territory shall have penetrated her vast domain and unsealed her now silent and unopened treasure houses; when immigration has cultivated and developed her resources; when men have peopled her waste places and have been rewarded by contact with her rich soil, the world will call a blooming garden what it once mistook for a wilderness of thorns.

CITY DIRECTORY.

A

Abramowsky, Julius, 11 Sixth st., M. Barash & Co.

Abeita, Pilar, 55 Plaza, clerk.

Adams, S. F., 3 Lincoln st., east.

Albright, J. M., residence 713 Grand ave., carpenter.

Albert & Herber, 8 south Sixth st., saloon proprietors.

Alvey, J. M., 137 Bridge st., printer.

Allen, C. F., residence 729 Grand ave., tinner.

Allen, Charles, 327 Grand ave., tinner.

Allison, Clarence, 12 Sixth st., clerk.

Amego, P., 33 Plaza, porter.

Anderson, Wm., 116 Sixth st.

Anderson, Thomas, 116 Sixth st.

Anderson, Julius, 10 Lincoln st., east, proprietor Globe saloon.

Andrews, Joe, 137 Bridge st., printer.

Armstrong, W., 224 Railroad ave., waiter.

Arey, A. R., 113½ Douglas, west, mattress manufacturer.

Asbridge, T. A., residence 108 Fifth st., contractor and builder.

Ash & Co., 419 Grand ave., gents' furnishing goods.

A. O. U. W., hall 13½ Sixth st.

B

Barton, J. W., residence 126 Fourth st.

Barton, J. W., residence 121 Fifth st.

Barton, Frank W., residence 121 Fifth st.

Baldonada, F., 16 Sixth st., porter.

Baker & Co., Mrs. J. B., 28 Sixth st., ladies' notions.

Baker, Miss Ida, 28 Sixth st., Mrs. J. B. Baker & Co.

Baker, J. B., 116 Seventh st., contractor and builder.

Buck, O., 112 Bridge st., proprietor Gallinas saloon.

Blackburne, B. F., residence 17 Railroad ave.

Bradley, D. W., residence 124 Railroad ave., carpenter.

Bently, Jessie, 226 Railroad ave.

Bell, John, 226 Railroad ave.

Brooks, Charles, 302 Railroad ave., cook.

Bartlett, C. H., 324 Railroad ave., jeweler.

Block & Co., 328 Railroad ave., gents' furnishing goods.

Block, I., 328 Railroad ave., Block & Co.

Barash, M. & Co., 11 Sixth st., dry goods and clothing.

Blakely, & Hand, 410 Railroad ave., proprietors saloon.

Bronson, A., 430 Railroad ave., carpenter.

Beebe, James, residence 618 Railroad ave., carpenter.

Bronson, A., residence 2 Washington, east, carpenter.

Browne & Manzanares, Lincoln, east of Railroad ave.

Boucher, S. P., residence 6 Washington, east, conductor.

Best & Treverton, 15 Tilden, east, carpenters and builders.

Browne, Jr., J. E., 127 Bridge st., proprietors Bridge fruit stand.

Browne, James, 137 Bridge st., printer.

Burnett & Co., J. E., 159½ Bridge st.

Blanchard, Charles, 3 Plaza, general merchandise.

Benitez, F., 41 Plaza.

Brownlee, Winters & Co., 43 Plaza, druggists.

Brownlee, J. D., 43 Plaza, Brownlee, Winters & Co.

Bernard, O. H., 10 and 12 Plaza, clerk.

Burton, Will C., 16 Plaza, proprietor Billy's saloon.

Bowler, Julia, 46 Plaza, chambermaid.

Bell & Co., 18 Sixth st., 50 Plaza, Plaza grocers.

Bell, H. C., 50 Plaza, Bell & Co., Plaza grocers.

Brash, B., 6 Sixth st., clerk.

Bishop, Mrs. M. S., 131 Grand ave.

Biglow, Mrs. Maria, 415½ Grand ave., confectioner.

Blake, J. C., 166 Bridge st., harness maker.

Burcher, J., F., 433 Grand ave., cigars and liquor agent,

Bigelow, Mrs. H. S., residence 126 Fourth st.

Bennett, N. A., residence 302 Fourth st., mechanic.

Blackwell, A. M., residence 120 Fifth st., commission merehant.

Bond, W. H., residence 309 Fifth st.

Burnett & Lyon, 22 Sixth st, plumbers.

Boeckelman, Louis, 13 Sixth st., book-keeper.

Berstler, George C., 216 Sixth st.

Browning, C. R., 11 Lincoln, real estate and insurance.

Bower, Fred, 152 Bridge st., residence 322 Seventh st.

Bostwick, J. F., 7 Douglas, attorney, residence 407 Seventh st.

Bostwick, Wm., C., residence 407 Seventh st.

Bostwick, Anna E., residence 407 Seventh st.

Brown, D. M., residence 421 Eighth st., minister.

Bogue, H. C., residence 511 Eighth st., railroad conductor.

Bloomer, D. F., 12½ Lincoln, east, barber.

Benton, H., 16 Lincoln, east.

Blood, D. A, residence 18 Gallinas st.

Booth, G. C., residence 117 and 119 Tilden st., superintendent street railroad.

Burdick, M. S., residence 123 Tilden st., laborer.

Beck, Byron, residence 1 and 3 Douglas, west, hotel waiter.

Burlingame, Wm., 1 and 3 Douglas, west, hotel clerk.

Bostwick & Whitelaw, 7 Douglas, west, attorneys.

Brown & Steele, 13 Douglas, west, insurance and real estate.

Brown, H. P., residence 213 Main, west.

Barney, J. W., residence 1 Douglas, east, proprietor Optic block.

Bromagen, J. C., residence 11 Douglas, east, printer.

Bower, Miss Lena, residence 316 Main, west.

Brown, S. T. H., residence 505 Blanchard, railroad conductor.

84   LAS VEGAS DIRECTORY.

C

Crary, A. B., 419½ Grand ave..

Clay, T. F., 625 Grand ave., expressman.

Christal, J. W., residence 22 Grand ave., engineer.

Carruth, J. A., residence 207 Fifth st.

Coxe, M. A., 431½ Grand ave., Optic office.

Carruth & Layton, Douglas, bet. Grand ave. and Sixth st., book and job printers.

Cunningham, G., 154 Bridge st., insurance agent.

Colville, James, 10 Sixth st., butcher, residence 210 Main, west.

Chamberlain & Newland, 154 Bridge st., jewelers.

Central office Bell Telephone Co., 11½ Sixth st.

Carpenter, George R., 116 Sixth st.

Cohenour, J. N., residence 313 Seventh st.

Campbell, W. P., residence 419 Eighth st., printer.

Conger, Del., residence 511 Eighth st., brakeman.

Carroll, J. H., residence 514 Eighth st., painter.

Collins, T. F., 9 Lincoln, east, proprietor saloon.

Carter, Green, 17 Lincoln, east, cook.

Cone, Charles D., 154 Bridge st., book-keeper.

Cameron, J. H., 2 Lincoln, east, Turf Exchange.

Conley, Charles, 2 Lincoln, east.

Chenoweth, L. W., 6 Lincoln, east.

Cooper, Walter, 18 Lincoln, east, confectioner.

Cowgar, A., residence 10 Gallinas st., railroad engineer.

Cornish, G. J., residence 122 Tilden, west.

Cameron, J. A., residence 132 Tilden, west.

Coors, W. F., 3 and 5 Lincoln, west, clerk.

Coors, Henry, Lockhart & Co., 3 and 5 Lincoln, west

Campos, Nat., 3 and 5 Lincoln, west, clerk.

Collier, David, 1 and 3 Douglas, west, hotel porter.

Campbell, E. M., 13 Douglas, west, attorney.

Cox, A. P. H., 206 Douglas, west, tinner.

Crusins, D. H., 206 Douglas, west, tinner.

Cook & Son, 18 Douglas, east, City livery stable.

Colville, David, residence 210 Main, west.

Cooley, P. L., residence 317 Main, west, railroad conductor.

Calhoun, Matt, 148 Bridge st., Calhoun & Heap.

Cunningham, W. O., residence 312 Main, west, real estate agent.

Calhoun & Heap, 148 Bridge st., real estate and live stock dealers.

Cavanaugh, M. J., residence 501 Blanchard, west, contractor and builder.

Carr & Fisher, 228 Railroad ave., proprietors Delaware house.

Carr, F. J., 228 Railroad ave., Carr & Fisher.

Cole, L. & Co., 314 Railroad ave., proprietors California chop house and saloon,

Cutter, F. W., 316 Railroad ave., clerk.

Coghlan, P., 332 Railroad ave., proprietor City shoe store.

Culp, G. A., 402 Railroad ave., tinner.

Conley, Jim, 406 Railroad ave., Fowler & Conley.

Carries, John C., residence 522 Railroad ave., shoemaker.

Case, C. E., 143½ Bridge st., barber.
Carroll, John, 39 Plaza, bartender.
Coghlan, P., 53 Plaza, Plaza furnishing store.
Crawford, A. J., 53 Plaza.
Cotter, Harry, 16 Plaza, bartender.
Commercial Dining Hall, 34 Plaza.
Colgan, Neal, 110 Bridge st., pawnbroker and second hand store.

D

Daniels, Russ, 413 Grand ave., cigar dealer.
Day, James, 701 Grand ave., carpenter and builder.
Danziger, Mrs. A., residence 4 Fifth st.
Duncan, J. S., residence 112 Fifth st., railroad contractor.
Duran, J., residence 424 Fifth st.
Danver, C. W., 15 Sixth st., gents' furnishing goods.
Daniel, Rup., 116 Sixth st.
Daley, D. W., 116 Sixth st., Daley & McKay.
Dacy, James, residence 220 Sixth st., carpenter.
Dyer, Charles, residence 404 Sixth st., railroad train master.
Decker, Wm., residence 508 Seventh st., railroad clerk.
Davidson, W., residence 424 Eighth st.
Davis, W., 3 Lincoln, east, clerk.
Danziger, A., 7 Lincoln, east, clerk.
Daigger, B., residence 106 Tilden, west, wagon maker.
Des Rocher, H., residence 118 Tilden, west, carpenter.
Davis, Alfred, 1 Lincoln, west, druggist.
De Lacy, Wm., 3 and 5 Lincoln, west, book-keeper.
Donovan, Frank, 1 and 3 Douglas, west, waiter.
Delaney, Thomas, 9 Douglas, east, proprietor Delaney house.
Douglas House, 17 Douglas, east, Mrs. M. Green, proprietress.
Duncan, J. M., residence 519 Blanchard, west.
Dean, Harry, 410 Railroad ave.
Dresser, J. T., residence 504 Railroad ave.
Day, George, residence 2 Gallinas, tie contractor.
Danver, George M., 15 Sixth st., clerk.
Davis, Joe, 302 Railroad ave., waiter.
Dobriner, Z., 33 Plaza, book-keeper.
Delgado, Martin, 51 Plaza, clerk.
Dinkel, George J., 2 Plaza, cashier.
Dunham & Co., 46 Plaza, proprietors Exchange hotel.

E

Evans, F. E., 311 Grand ave., photographer.
Ellis, L. H., 17 Douglas, west, sign painter.
Edwards, Dr. G P., 5 Douglas, east.
Edwards, Richard, 420 Railroad ave
Enlich, P. M., 145½ Bridge st., tobacconist.
Elsworth, W. F., 51 Plaza, book-keeper.

F

French, P. W., residence 621 Railroad ave., auctioneer.
Fowler & Conley, 406 Railroad ave., proprietors saloon.
Furnald, L. H., 310 Railroad ave., clerk.
Fisher, B. F., residence 228 Railroad ave.
Fort, L. C., residence 517 Blanchard, west, lawyer.
Fuller, Bert, 17 Douglas, east, cook.
Follett, George A., 201 Grand ave.
Fisk, Calvin, 433½ Grand ave., real estate broker.
Fiskel, H. H., residence 525 Grand ave., clerk
Fox, W., residence 717 Grand ave.
Foster, J. W., residence 106 Fourth st.
Fowler, W. L., residence 308 Fourth st., contractor.
Fox, W., 10 Sixth st., meat cutter.
Fabian, W. & Co., 16 Sixth st., wholesale liquor dealer.
Flower, E. W., 116 Sixth st.
Fort, L. C., 114 Eighth st., lawyer.
Frommouth, Louis, 8 Lincoln, east, barkeeper.
Fritsch, F. A., 11 Lincoln, west, clerk.
Fonner, J. P., residence 212 Lincoln, west.
Falk, Henry, 4½ Douglas, west, meat cutter.
Finane & Elston, 17 Douglas, west, painters.
Ford, Mrs. Mary P., residence 1 and 3 Douglas, west, clerk.
Fleming, J., 109 Douglas, west, plumber.
Fleming, A., 109 Douglas, west, plumber.
Fox, Mrs. L. S., residence 215 Douglas, west.
Fitzgerrell, J. J., 405 Grand ave., real estate agent.
Furlong, & Ticer, 131 Bridge st., stationers.
Furlong, J. M., 131 Bridge st., postmaster, Furlong & Ticer.
Fleming, P. A., 145 Bridge st., clerk.
Farley, J., 11 Plaza, clerk.
First National Bank, 2 Plaza.
Frey, Robert, 132 Bridge st., cabinet-maker.
Fleming, S. J., 154 Bridge st., on Mining World.

G

Gray, Sam, residence 4 Third st., carpenter.
Goldberg, D., 10½ Sixth st., pawnbroker.
Goldberg, L., 10½ Sixth st., clerk.
Gross, J., 24 Sixth st., Gross, Blackwell & Co., residence 309 Seventh st.
Gray, Arthur, 116 Sixth st.
Grant, K. T., 116 Sixth st.
Gazelle, Charles, 116 Seventh st., carpenter.
Gray, John W., residence 6 Eighth st., mason.
Gregory & Williams, 19 Lincoln, east, proprietors barber shop.
Gascoigne, John, residence 5 Prince, west, carpenter.
Gallegher, William, residence 31 Gallinas st., carpenter.
Gordon, Dr. C. C., residence and office 3 Douglas, east.

Green, A. G., 15 Douglas, east, city painter.
Green, Mrs. M., 17 Douglas, east, proprietress Douglas house.
Goodwin, Mrs., residence 220 Railroad ave., cook.
Gentle, Charles, 224 Railroad ave , proprietor Kansas dining hall.
Gentle, James, 224 Railroad ave., clerk.
Grant, R. P., 33 Plaza, clerk.
Gray, Richard, 226 Railroad ave., dish washer.
Grogan, C. P., 316 Railroad ave., clerk.
Graaf, J., 145 Bridge st., Weil & Graaf.
Guerin, Miguel, 11 Plaza, cashier.
Goldsmith, L. R., 10 and 12 Plaza, clerk.
Gates, Thomas, 46 Plaza, cook.
Gray, W. H., 132 Bridge st., clerk.
Griswold & Murphy, 174 Bridge st., druggists.
Gazette, 137 Bridge st., J. H. Koogler, proprietor.

H

Holland, Mose, residence 227 Grand ave., laborer.
Hopkins, S. J., 313 Grand ave., millinery and fancy goods.
Hornbarger, O. B., residence 114 Grand ave.
Herrington, J. S., residence 4 Third st., carpenter.
Hart, M. S., residence 411 Fifth st., superintendent gas works.
Huberty, Henry, residence 423 Fifth st.
Hill, Frank A., 14 Sixth st., agent Adams Express Co.
Hadley, Walter C., 16½ Sixth st., notary public, rooms 1 and 2.
Hendriks, H. D., 18 Sixth st., clerk.
Hawkins, Fred, 22 Sixth st., clerk.
Hood, A. G., 24 Sixth st., book-keeper San Miguel National bank.
Hoskins, D. P., 24 Sixth st., clerk for San Miguel National bank.
Hennigar, J. F., 116 Sixth st.
Hennigar, A. G., 116 Sixth st.
Holman, Flocy, residence 210 Sixth st.
Hunter, Robert H., residence 222 Sixth st.
Henriques, Dr., residence 306 Sixth st.
Holmes, R. J., residence 319 Seventh st., ice dealer.
Hovey, C. P., residence 318 Seventh st., Railroad and Wells Fargo agent.
Huberty & Angell, 5 Lincoln, east, bakery and lunch.
Hayward Bros., 13 Lincoln, east, butchers.
Hodgson, Prof. H. F., residence Gallinas st., musician.
Hollingworth, C., residence 110 Tilden, west, carpenter.
Herbert, Eugene, residence 101 Tilden, west.
Hibbs, William P., residence 109 Tilden, west, City laundry.
Hopkins, Mrs. E. A., residence 115 Tilden, west.
Hine & Schaefer, 3 Lincoln, east, druggists.
Henry, E., 11 Lincoln, west, insurance agent.
Hendricks, Arthur, 1 and 3 Douglas, west, third cook.
Hedgecock, Charles, 11 Douglas, west.
Harlan, Charles, 17 Douglas, west, paper hanger.

Howard, J. M. D., residence 129 Railroad ave.
Howard, Rincy, residence 129 Railroad ave., carpenter.
Holstein, Sim, 1 and 3 Douglas, west, cattle dealer.
Hutton, Mrs. Maggie, 101 Douglas, west, laundress.
Harbaugh, James, 204 Douglas, west, tinner.
Himrod, S. A , residence 215 Main, west, civil engineer,
Higgins, A. D., residence 315 Main, west, book-keeper.
Heap, Clarence, residence 306 Main, west, Calhoun & Heap, real estat agents.
Harkey, L. C., residence 7 Blanchard, west.
Harvey, Mrs. R. A., residence 7 Blanchard, west.
Hixon, William, residence 210 Blanchard, west.
House, W. L., residence 9 Washington, west, carpenter.
Halterbran, J. H., residence 13 Washington, west, teamster.
Hudson, William, 226 Railroad ave., American house.
Harlow, Wm., 226 Railroad ave.
Harlow, George, 226 Railroad ave.
Hall, Charles, 226 Railroad ave.
Hayden, Joseph, 226½ Railroad ave., barber shop.
Hunter, W. E., 226½ Railroad ave., barber.
Heizer, Richard, 226½ Railroad ave., barber.
Holmes, V. E., 312 Railroad ave., merchant tailor.
Hopper Bros., 316 Railroad ave., groceries and provisions.
Hawkins, J. K., 316 Railroad ave., clerk.
Hoffner, John, 316 Railroad ave., clerk.
Hayden, Joe, 318 Railroad ave., barkeeper.
Harper, Tom, 318 Railroad ave., barkeeper.
Hoagland, H. J., 324 Railroad ave., jeweler.
Howison, L. L., 332 Railroad ave., manager City shoe store.
Houghton, O. L., 402 Railroad ave., and 28 Plaza, hardware.
Hoffmeaster, Charles, 404½ Railroad ave.
Hand, J. W.. 410 Railroad ave., Blakely & Hand.
Hayen, Barbara, residence 420 Railroad ave., chambermaid.
Hilton, Charles W., residence 612 Railroad ave., mason.
Hobbs, O. H., residence 802 Railroad ave., clerk.
Hesser, R. P., residence 408 Main, west, painter.
Heise & Straus, 135 Bridge st., wholesale liquor dealers.
Hogsett, P. C., 11 Plaza, clerk.
Hubbell, W. B., 39 Plaza, clerk.
Haynes, W. H., 39 Plaza, bartender.
Heinke, Wm., 39 Plaza.
Hunter, J., 39 Plaza.
Harris, S., 47 Plaza, staple and fancy groceries.
Hoffman, W., 110 Bridge st., clerk.
Harry, Wm., 152 Bridge st., meat cutter.

I

I. O. O. F., Fraternity Hall, 13½ Sixth st.
Ilfeld, Charles, 31 Plaza, general merchandise.

J

Johnson, Ben, 26 Plaza, butcher.
Jackson, J. M., 137 Bridge st., job printer.
Johnson, H. W., 18 Sixth st., clerk.
Joy, H. C., 116 Sixth st.
Johnson, B. E., 116 Sixth st
Johnson, Ed, 116 Sixth st.
Jonas, D. D., 23 Seventh st., harness maker.
Jewell, Clayton B., residence 511 Eighth st., clerk.
Johnson, B. E., residence 510 Eighth st., clerk.
Jennison, Homer L., 16 Lincoln, east, bartender, residence 11 Blanchard, east.
Johnston, R., residence 108 Tilden, west, carpenter.
Jarvis, W. L., residence 125 Tilden, west, blacksmith.
Joly, D., 4½ Douglas, west, proprietor Union meat market.
Jennings, Miss Belle, 1 and 3 Douglas, west, clerk.
Jerrell, C. C., residence 221 Douglas, west, carpenter.
Jaffa Bros., 330 Railroad ave., dry goods and clothing.
Jaffa, N., 330 Railroad ave., clerk.
Jameson, J. A., 21 Bride st., clerk.

K

Kauffman, S. & Co., 407 Grand ave., grocers.
K. of P., 13½ Sixth st., Fraternity Hall.
Keen, A. A., residence 319 Sixth st.
Knobb, William, 1 Lincoln, west, shoemaker, residence 621 Grand ave.
Knell, H., 9 Lincoln, west, bartender.
Knapp, D. S., residence 126 Tilden, west, engineer.
Kee, Hop, 15 Douglas, west, Chinese laundry.
Keller & Clemm, 101 Douglas, west, proprietors St. Nicholas hotel.
Kruding, Mrs. Herman, 206 Douglas, west, millinery and fancy goods.
Kruding, Herman, residence 206 Douglas, west, mason.
Keesee, William, residence 19 Douglas, east, blacksmith, shop 434 Railroad ave.
Keever, John, 314 Railroad ave., cook.
Koebele, Peter, residence 526 Railroad ave., cook.
Klatteneoff, J. B., 17 Bridge st., furniture dealer.
Kester, William, 5 Lincoln, east, baker.
Krouch, George, 17 Lincoln, east, second cook.
Koogle, A. C., residence 637 Railroad ave.
Koogler, J. H., 137 Bridge st., proprietor Daily Gazette.
Koogler, W. G., 137 Bridge st., city editor Daily Gazette.
Koogler, A. W., 137 Bridge st., preesman Daily Gazette.
Keen, A. A., 2 Plaza, clerk.
Kaufmann, B., 10 and 12 Plaza, clerk.
Kaufmann, M., 10 and 12 Plaza, clerk.
Kelley, Alexander, 32 Plaza, Rawlins & Kelley.
Kinlock, J. G., 48 Plaza, bartender.
Kistler, R. A., 431½ Grand ave, proprietor Daily Optic.
Kistler, W. D., 431½ Grand ave., business manager Daily Optic.

L

Lowe, John H., residence 27 Grand ave., engineer.
Lockhart & Co., 325 and 327 Grand ave., paint and tin shop 3 & 5 Lincoln, west.
Larson, C. J., 409 Grand ave., merchant tailor.
Lisenbee, Mrs. N. E., 415 Grand ave., millinery and fancy goods.
Lowe, Annie, residence 114 Grand ave.
Levy, Edward, 16 Sixth st., traveling agent.
Liddell, Van R., residence 224 Sixth st.
Liddell, F. R., residence 224 Sixth st.
Lease, George, 411 Seventh st., conductor.
Lee & Fort, 114 Eighth st., attorneys at law.
Lee, Wm. D., residence 118 Eighth st., attorney.
Lyons, J. W., residence 424 Eighth st., contractor and builder.
Lane, Andrew 17 Lincoln, east, waiter.
Locke & Bond, 16 Lincoln, east, proprietors Locke's saloon.
Leibschner, Charles, residence 111 Tilden, west, butcher.
Lee, Sam, 19 Lincoln, west, Chinese laundry.
Lehman, Cy., 11 Douglas, west.
Lee, John, 7 Douglas, east, Chinese laundry.
Law, M. J., residence 11 Blanchard, west.
Lucero, F., residence 513 Blanchard, west.
Lee, Sing, 220½ Railroad ave., Chinese laundry.
Lipsey, S. H., 224 Railroad ave., waiter.
Lawton, R. A., 226 Railroad ave.
Lewis, William, 302 Railroad ave., dish washer.
Lewis, Isaac, 312 Railroad ave., Golden Rule furnishing store.
Lum, Chancy, residence 614 Railroad ave., carpenter.
Lehman, D. I., residence 805 Railroad ave., carpenter.
Liddell, C. M., residence 224 Sixth st., carpenter.
Lake, Mrs. H. E., 5 Douglas, west, dressmaker.
Laughlin, John O., 222 Railroad ave., bartender.
Lydon, P. O , 133½ Bridge st., attorney.
Lytton, Charles E., 137 Bridge st., city circulator Daily Gazette.
Lockhart, J. A., residence 223 Main, west.
Leduc, Frank, 143 Bridge st., merchant tailor.
Leon Bros., 33 Plaza, bakery, groceries and provisions.
Lemke, A , 45 Plaza, wholesale liquors and tobaccos.
Lord, S,, 108 Bridge st., tinner.
Levy, H., 6 Sixth st., proprietor New York clothing store.

M

Matzen & Co., 411 Grand ave,, restaurant and bakery.
Marcus, M. D., residence 521 Grand ave., store 7 Lincoln, east.
McNamee, John, 601 Grand ave., blacksmith.
Mitchell, Dr. G. W., residence 727 Grand ave.
Martin, M., residence 118 Grand ave.
Mason. S. E., 202 Grand ave.

Martin & French, 402 Grand ave. and 1 Sixth st , auctioneers.
McKinney, George, residence 8 Fifth st., saloonist.
McNair, T. B., residence 114 Fifth st.
Mills, Irve, 11½ Sixth st., superintendent Bell Telephone Co.
Martinez, Felix, 13 Sixth st , general merchandise, res. 515 Blanchard st.
McKay, George, 116 Sixth st., Daley & McKay, proprietors Grand Central.
Moss, C. M., residence 224 Sixth st.
McCormic, J. E., residence 224 Sixth st., brakeman.
Malboeuf, Wm., 23 Seventh st., harness maker.
McConnell, F. W., residence 468 Seventh st., carpenter.
McConnell, J. E., residence 422 Seventh st., carpenter.
Marble, H., residence 508 Seventh st., conductor.
Marble, Fred, residence 503 Seventh st., brakeman.
Methodist Episcopal Church, 425 Seventh st.
Mitchell, L., residence 409 Tenth st.
Maley, John, 13 Lincoln, east, butcher.
Marble, W. E., 17 Lincoln, east, restaurant, residence 115 Main.
Milligan, M. M., M. D., office 4 Lincoln, east.
McIntire & Johnson, 14 Lincoln, east, proprietors Railroad saloon.
Morehouse, Charles, residence 10 Gallinas st., fireman.
McIntire, residence 7 Gallinas st.
Maynard, A., residence 120 Tilden, west, machanic.
Mackel, C. B., residence 212 Tilden, west, shoemaker.
Means, John B., 13 Douglas, west, clerk.
Meyers, J. F., 101 Douglas, west, bartender.
Manning, Richard, 109 Douglas, west, plumber.
Marsh, William H., 204 Douglas, west, tinner.
McKinney, Dr. T. A , 205 Douglas, west, eclectic physician.
Miller, W. E., residence 221 Douglas, west.
Marshall, W. T., residence 210 Main, west.
Moore, M. A., residence 302 Main, west.
Marsh, Oliver, residence 317 Washington, west, lumber dealer.
Melindy, Charles, 220 Railroad ave., proprietor Valley saloon.
Maxwell, M. A., 1 and 3 Douglas, west, proprietors Sumner house.
Montgomery, Richard, 226 Railroad ave., cook.
Montgomery, Nellie, 226 Railroad ave.
McConnell, Oscar, 318 Railroad ave., proprietor Arcade saloon.
Michael, Wm. M., 326 Railroad ave., clerk.
Morcuse, L. J., 328 Railroad ave., clerk.
Martinez, Moderto, 334 Railroad ave., porter.
McCrum, S., 402 Railroad ave , clerk.
Miller, R. W., 414 Railroad ave., proprietor Comique.
Marleman, Charles, 420 Railroad ave.
Mimium, J., 426 Railroad ave , wool grader.
Morgan, D., 432 Railroad ave., carpenter.
McKechen, D. A., residence 812 Railroad ave., carpenter.
Mendenhall, Hunter & Co., 427 Grand ave., East Side livery stable.
McNulty, P. J., 1 and 3 Douglas, west, contractor and builder.

Marshall, Alex., residence 210 Main, west.
McCurdy, James, 420 Railroad ave., proprietor Topeka house.
Marwede, Brumley & Co., 133 Bridge st., hardware.
Moriarty, Thomas, 3 Plaza, clerk.
McCleary, Miss E., 11 Plaza, clerk.
Myer, Frank, 21 Plaza, butcher.
Morley, Mrs., 39 Plaza.
Meastes, Jose M., 55 Plaza, clerk.
Moss, W. L., 2 Plaza, clerk.
Marcellino, Boffa & Perez, 4 Plaza, fruit dealers; 8 Plaza, music hall.
Mould, W. W., 16 Plaza, cook.
Martin, P. J., 146 Bridge st., proprietor Chapman hall.
Mills, T. B., 154 Bridge st., real estate, insurance and mining agent.

N

Nelson, Philip, 409½ Grand ave., liquor and tobacco.
Nelson, Kate, 6½ Lincoln, east, proprietress restaurant.
Nicholas, J. A., residence 10 Eighth st.
Netterberg, 302 Railroad ave., proprietor New York house.
Nenfeld, H. J., 326 Railroad ave., clerk.
Nalun, S., 336 Railroad ave., clerk.

O

Optic Office, 431½ Grand ave., R. A. Kistler, proprietor.
Oakley, Robert, 16 Sixth st., W. Fabian & Co., residence 521 Blanchard, west.
O'Kane, William, 18 Sixth st., clerk.
Otero, M. A., 24 Sixth st., president San Miguel National bank, residence 307 ↓ Main, west.
Ortego, Pedro, 13 Sixth st., clerk.
Oldham, Ralph, 5 Lincoln, east.
O'Neal, James, residence 116 Tilden, west, fireman.
Olemar, Nick, residence 212 Tilden, west, shoemaker.
O'Bryn, W. S., residence 215 Tilden, west, laborer.
Otero, Jr., M. A., residence 303 Main, west.
Overhuls, J. H., residence 321 Washington, west, lumber merchant.
Oppenheim, A., 404½ Railroad ave., clerk.
Oudkerk, H., 165 Bridge st., merchant tailor.
Overman, Frank, 137 Bridge st., assistant pressman on Daily Gazette.

P

Plaza hotel, 39 Plaza, Mrs. S. B. Davis, proprietress.
Plaza billiard hall, 37 Plaza.
Prentice & Schleifer, 417 Grand ave., butchers.
Page, Mr., residence 114 Grand ave.
Planert, Henry H., 10 Sixth st., grocer.
Pierce, Richard C., 14 Sixth st., Adams Express driver.
Ponder, John H., 22 Sixth st., plumber.
Palmar, J. H., 22 Sixth st., plumber.

Armijo Bros. & Borradaile take full charge of Properties, pay and collect Rents.

LAS VEGAS DIRECTORY. 93

Powers, M. J., 23 Seventh st., harness maker.
Pishon, J. S., residence 319 Seventh st.
Phillips, Harry, 17 Lincoln, east, waiter.
Phillips & Milligan, 4 Lincoln, east, fancy groceries, cigars and tobacco.
Porter, Gay E., 4 Lincoln, east, real estate and collecting agent.
Potter, F. W., 106 Railroad ave., lumber merchant, residence 5 Tilden, west.
Prentice, C. A., residence 113 Tilden, west, butcher.
Prichard, G. W., 5½ Lincoln, west, attorney, residence 315 Main, west
Prindle, John R., 1 and 3 Douglas, west, cook.
Prikal, Frank, 204 Douglas, west, tinner.
Parsons, Mrs. Eva, residence 116 Blanchard, west.
Price, C J., 316 Railroad ave., clerk.
Parsons, C. A., 332 Railroad ave., clerk.
Pyle, J. T., 430 Railroad ave., carpenter.
Pearce, J. W., 432 Railroad ave., repair shop.
Powell, R., residence 626 Railroad ave.
Potter, F. L., 106 Railroad ave., teamster.
Preston, C., 432 Railroad ave., carpenter.
Post Office, 131 Bridge st., J. N. Furlong, Postmaster.
Paxson, E. C., 135 Bridge st., clerk.
Pigeon, E., 3 Plaza, clerk.
Parsons, C A., 53 Plaza.
Pashon, J. S., 2 Plaza, assistant cashier First National bank.
Patty, S., 108 Bridge st., dealer in tinware and stoves.

Q

Quigley, Mrs. Mary, residence 29 Gallinas st.
Quinn, John, residence 725 Railroad ave., laborer.
Quisenberry, A. L., 11 Lincoln, west, clerk.

R

Rutenbeck, Theodore, 150 Bridge st., dealer in cigars and tobacco.
Rankin, Will., residence 114 Grand ave.
Reed, G. W., residence 120 Grand ave., oil agent.
Reed, Overton, residence 122 Grand ave.
Roberts, J. C., residence 124 Grand ave., baggage-master.
Rupe & Bullard, 302 Grand ave., lumber yard and plaining mill.
Ross, Vina, residence 2 Fourth st., wood dealer.
Robosser, John, residence 6 Fifth st., carpenter.
Rhoads, Charles L., 14 Sixth st., Adams Express clerk.
Reilley, J. E., 24 Sixth st., teller San Miguel National bank.
Russell, J. D., 26 Sixth st., Sweet & Co.
Rust, Dr. D. H., 11½ Sixth st., dentist.
Robbins, W B., 116 Sixth st.
Reinohl, J. D., residence 21 Seventh st., tinner.
Reinohl, A. W., residence 21 Seventh st., carpenter.
Richards, Charles, 411 Seventh st., conductor.
Rees, Mrs., S. E., residence 118 Eighth st.

Rathbun, C. A., 1 Lincoln, east, boots, shoes and gents' furnishing goods ; 139 Bridge st., boot and shoe shop.

Reidlinger, Jacob, 4½ Lincoln, east, barber ; hot and cold baths ; residence 217 Douglas, west.

Romero, Damasio, 14 Lincoln, east, bartender.

Rogers, Samuel, residence 35 Gallinas, st.

Rountree, Jr., G., residence 209 Tilden, west, clerk.

Robbins, Dr. M. W., 5½ Lincoln, west.

Rosenwald, J., 24 Sixth st., vice-president San Miguel National bank.

Rawlins, W. W., 48 Plaza, proprietor Exchange saloon.

Rodgers, James, 110 Bridge st., clerk.

Reck, Louis, 101 Douglas, west, cook.

Riordan, Wm., 110 Bridge st.

Roberts, Henry, 101 Douglas, west, second cook.

Rountree, B. C., 318 Main, west, grocer.

Ruby, E., residence 214 Blanchard, west.

Romero, Mrs. R. B., residence 513 Blanchard, west.

Ricker, John, 226 Railroad ave.

Russell, E. E., 132 Bridge st., clerk.

Richman, K. C., 324 Railroad ave., jeweler.

Rosenthal, N. L., 326 Railroad ave., general merchandise.

Rosenthal, Charles, 326 Railroad ave., clerk.

Rosenthal, Saul, 326 Railroad ave., clerk.

Rosenthal, Wm., 326 Railroad ave., clerk.

Riedlinger Bros., 412 Railroad ave., proprietors Las Vegas beer garden

Ryan & Robbins, 430 Railroad ave., carpenters.

Robbins Ed, 430 Railroad ave., Ryan & Robbins.

Rodan & Salter, 109 Bridge st., proprietors McBrayer saloon.

Robbins, A. O., 132 Bridge st., furniture and undertaker.

Rowe, S. M., residence 210 Lincoln, west, engineer.

Rowe, Robert D., residence 210 Lincoln, west, clerk.

Reeves, V. A., 17 Lincoln, east, clerk.

Rogers, Charles, residence 35 Gallinas st.

Rogers, Enoch, residence 35 Gallinas st.

Repeto, Joe, 412½ Railroad ave., Woods & Repeto.

Rolins, Frank, 137 Bridge st., printer.

Romero, H. & Bro., 11 Plaza, dealers in general merchandise.

Rodgers, Charles, 33 Plaza, baker.

Romero, M., 51 Plaza, general merchandise.

Romero, Miguel 51 Plaza, clerk.

Romero, Caunto, 51 Plaza, clerk.

Raynolds, J., 2 Plaza, president First National bank.

Robertson, John H., 2 Plaza, clerk.

Rosenwald, J., 10 and 12 Plaza, general merchandise.

Rawlins & Kelley, 32 Plaza, saloon proprietors.

Rawlins, William, 52 Plaza, Rawlins & Kelley.

Romero, T. & Son, 40 Plaza.

Robertson, J, H., 46 Plaza, steward.

S

Sylvester, Charles D., printer, 207 Fifth st.

Snarr, C. O., residence 19 Grand ave., carpenter.

Snarr, A. N., residence 19 Grand ave., carpenter.

Smmmerfield, Mrs. Dr. R., residence 2 Fifth st.

Stark, A. G., 12 Sixth st., commission merchant.

Sebben, E. W., 20 Sixth st., broker.

Sweet & C., 26 Sixth st., news and tobacco.

Smith, A. C., 21 Seventh st., blacksmith.

Seewald, W. H., 1 Lincoln, east, jeweler.

Samuel, E., 7 Lincoln, east, clerk.

Stone, A. B., residence 35 Gallinas st., carpenter.

Sumner House, 1 and 3 Douglas, west, Mrs. M. A. Maxwell.

Sumner, Mrs. George, 1 and 3 Douglas, west.

Stevenson, H. R., 1 and 3 Douglas, west, accountant.

Stire, H. G., 5 Douglas, west, millinery and fancy goods.

Steel, Wm., 13 Douglas, west, justice of the peace, residence 211 Main, west.

Smith, Miss Vina J., 1 and 3 Douglas, west, clerk at B. & M.'s.

St. Nicholas Hotel, 101 Douglas, west, Keller & Clemm, proprietors.

Steinbeck, William, 101 Douglas, west, pastry cook.

Shumaker, F. W., 204 Douglas, west, tinner.

Stockton, A. P., residence 103 Main, west.

Scrutton, Robert, residence 302 Main, west, railroad clerk.

Stewart, Mrs. J. P., residence 306 Main, west.

Studebaker, R., residence 308 Main, west, wool and hides.

Stewart, S. W., 324 Main, west, proprietors Stewart's boarding house.

Seely, T. J., residence 220 Blanchard, west, division sup't A., T. & S. F. R. R.

Stoneroad, N. B., residence 313 Inter-Ocean, west, sheep dealer.

Searight, C. C., 222 Railroad ave., proprietor Turf saloon.

Sullivan, Charles, 314 Railroad ave., L. Cole & Co.

Siegfried, C. A., 402 Railroad ave., clerk.

Sherwood, A., 434 Railroad ave., blacksmith.

Stanton, O. B., residence 522 Eighth st, railroad office.

Smith, George, 334 Railroad ave., bartender.

Strowbridge, Tona, 137 Bridge st., printer.

Shupp, W. H., 147 and 149 Bridge st., buggy and wagon maker.

Shield, D. P., 433½ Grand ave., attorney.

Schultz, F. H., 167 Bridge st., boot and shoe maker.

Senecal, A. A., 3 Plaza, clerk.

Scandinavian House, 13 Plaza.

Sandoval, F., y Baca, 23 Plaza, wines and liquors.

Schiller, Albert, 33 Plaza, baker.

Simpson, Harry A., 39 Plaza, clerk.

Shoemaker, Sam E., 43 Plaza, Brownlee, Winters & Co.

Smith, A. B., 2 Plaza, clerk.

Sena Bros., 42 Plaz, dealers in general merchandise.

Sena, Partricio, 42 Plaza, clerk.

Smith, Minnie, 46 Plaza, waiter.
Smith, Anderson, 46 Plaza, waiter.
Stewart, Oscar, 46 Plaza, dish-washer,
Schuster, Emery, 46 Plaza, assistant dish-washer.
Sing, Sam, 130½ Bridge st., Chinese laundry.
Sandoval, Adolfo, 11 Plaza, clerk.
Stern, Isidor, 36 Plaza, dealer in general merchandise.
San Miguel National Bank, 29 Sixth st.
Shiner, E. S., residence 620 Railroad ave.
Schultz, F. H., residence 634½ Railroad ave., shoemaker.
Skinner, Mrs. H. L., residence 917 Railroad ave.
Stern, I., residence 5 Bridge st., merchant.
Staltz & Probst, 408 Grand ave., proprietors East Side news stand.
Summers, J. D., residence 114 Grand ave., telegraph operator.
Seewald, W. H., residence 316 Seventh st., jeweler.

T

Trainer, L. E., residence 203 Grand ave., engineer.
Taylor, S. M., residence 306 Fourth st., carpenter.
Thomas, T. M., 116 Sixth st., waiter.
Tingley, John, residence 8 Eighth st., teamster.
Talbott, T. J., 7 Lincoln, east, clerk.
Torah, James, 7 Lincoln, east, porter.
Toft, Charles, 10 Lincoln, east, proprietor Globe saloon.
Toft, Andrew E., 10 Lincoln, east, bartender.
Trask, Wm. B., 12 Lincoln, east, proprietor Optic saloon.
Treverton, T, residence 104 Tilden, west, carpenter.
Taylor & Fowler, 23 Lincoln, west, builders.
Theobald, J. P., 11 Douglas, west, boot and shoe maker, res. 304 Main, west.
Taylor, Mrs. S. M., 304 Fourth st., private school.
Tamme, Charles, 334 Railroad ave., Ward & Tamme.
Talbott, T. J., residence 518 Railroad ave.
Tallman, rasidence 17 Bridge st., artist.
Tremble, S. M., 30 Plaza, proprietor Plaza restaurant.
Thornton, R., R., 154 Bridge st., architect and civil engineer.
Thorp, N. B. & Co., 172 Bridge st., groceries.

W

Woodson, Eran, 327½ Grand ave., proprietor Bachelor's hall.
Wing, Sing, 411½ Grand ave., Chinese laundry.
Wright, Charles, 6 Lincoln, east, proprietor Wright's place.
Wilkinson, George, residence 811 Grand ave., carpenter.
Wooster, C. A., residence 729½ Grand ave.
Wiegand, C., 102 Grand ave., proprietor soda works.
Wack, Fredric, residence 110 Grand ave., carpenter.
Whitmore, Adin H., 16½ Sixth st., room 1.
Weill, S., 330 Railroad ave., clerk.
Western Union Telegraph Office, 131½ Bridge st.

Whitney, William, 22 Sixth st., plumber.
Waite, W. D., 11 Sixth st., clerk.
Wisner, J. A., residence 208 Seventh st., conductor.
Wiley, C. W., residence 310 Seventh st., railroad contractor
Ward, John, residence 406 Seventh st.
Ward, J. H., residence 108 Eighth st , railroad contractor
White, Fred, 17 Lincoln, east, waiter.
Whitmore, J. J., 16 Lincoln, east.
Ward, W. D., residence 118 Tilden, west, painter.
Whitnah, M. P., residence 109½ Tilden, west.
White, Sam, residence 214 Tilden, west, expressman
Wise, A. A. and J. H., 9 Douglas, west, real estate and mining agents.
Wooster House, 517 Grand ave., W. H. Wooster, proprietor.
Whitney, George J., 101 Douglas, west, steward.
Williams, Mrs. H., 115½ Douglas, west.
Williford, Jay, 204 Douglas, west, cornice maker.
Watt, Jack, 204 Douglas, west.
Williamson, J. T., 207 Douglas, west, cook.
Willson, Joseph, residence 213 Douglas, west.
Waite, B. L., residence 219 Douglas, west
Wright, Nat, 130 Railroad ave., proprieror Nat Wright's place.
Whiteman, M., residence 306 Railroad ave
Williams, C. M., 310 Railroad ave., druggist.
Wade, John A., 332 Railroad ave., book-keeper.
Ware & Tamme, 334 Railroad ave., proprietors Monarch billiard hall.
Ward, G. W., 334 Railroad ave , Ward & Tamme.
Williams, W. M., 402 Railroad ave., foreman tin shop.
Wheelock, Charles, 133½ Bridge st., architect.
Weil & Graaf, 145 Bridge st., commission merchants.
Weil, A., 145 Bridge st., Weil & Graaf.
Winters, D. C., 43 Plaza, Brownlee, Winters & Co.
Wesche, C. E., 55 Plaza, general merchandise.
Walters, Albert, 46 Plaza, second cook.
Whitelaw, Frank, 433½ Grand ave., editor Fisk's Great Southwest.
Wilcox, Lute, 433 Grand ave., city editor Daily Optic.

Y

Young, Patrick, residence 309 Grand ave., clerk.
Young, William, 101 Douglas, west, dish-washer.
Yantis & Thompson, 133½ Bridge st., dentists.
Young, Miss S. T., 11 Plaza, clerk.